# THE SINGER ACTS, THE ACTOR SINGS

# THE SINGER ACTS, THE ACTOR SINGS

## A Practical Guide to Living Through Song, Vocally and Dramatically

GLENN SEVEN ALLEN

methuen | drama
LONDON • NEW YORK • OXFORD • NEW DELHI • SYDNEY

METHUEN DRAMA
Bloomsbury Publishing Plc
50 Bedford Square, London, WC1B 3DP, UK
1385 Broadway, New York, NY 10018, USA

BLOOMSBURY, METHUEN DRAMA and the Methuen Drama logo are trademarks of Bloomsbury Publishing Plc

First published in Great Britain 2019



Cover design: Holly Bell



A catalogue record for this book is available from the British Library.

A catalog record for this book is available from the Library of Congress.

ISBN: HB: 978-1-3500-4306-0
PB: 978-1-3500-4307-7
ePDF: 978-1-3500-4305-3
eBook: 978-1-3500-4308-4

Series: Performance Books

Typeset by Integra Software Services Pvt. Ltd.
Printed and bound in Great Britain

# CONTENTS

# FIGURES

# CONTRIBUTORS

Grace Field was a visual arts major in college and since then her work has been sold worldwide. She is thrilled to be the illustrator of this book; especially since Ms. Field is a musical theater performer as well! She has had the privilege of singing at the Lincoln Center, Broadway's New Victory Theater, and Off Broadway's June Havoc Theatre and has worked with Broadway's Stephen Schwartz, Anthony Rapp, and Rebecca Luker. She is currently a soloist for the United Nations headquarters in New York City and is also a member of Grammy-nominated Broadway choir Broadway Inspirational Voices. For more visit gracefield.net or follow @ thegracefield.

# PREFACE

As a young singer and actor, I was forever attempting to reconcile the binary nature of my training. As I heard them described, the art of singing and the art of acting seemed to be separate disciplines. In private voice lessons and group acting classes, rarely did anyone make clear to me how to combine the two. In search of answers, I scoured libraries and bookstores, where I discovered several wonderful books on the technique of singing, many on the technique of acting, and a few on auditioning for musical theater, but I never found one that addressed singing and acting together—or, more important, acting *while* singing.

But in my twenty-five years of training, performing, and teaching, I've had the privilege of dedicating my life to the art of living through song. I've had many opportunities to think about this unique art form and formulate my own approach to it. My experience—in musical theater, cabaret, opera, concerts, film, television, a cappella groups, and more—has culminated in this book, in which I share with you some concrete and *practical* guidance to help you think of the two disciplines as one. Whether you're an experienced singer looking for a simpler, clearer acting process or an actor who feels insecure about your singing abilities, this is the book for you—the book I wish I'd found when I began my journey as a singing actor.

A perfect symbol for what we're trying to accomplish by combining singing and acting is a strand of DNA. Picture it: two separate ribbons bound by a common purpose, spinning together harmoniously. One strand is acting: here we will dispel with the mysticism often associated with this art, instead focusing on building a strong technical foundation. This will be rooted in a specific and repeatable process that will unlock your body and imagination and free your inner storyteller. The second strand is singing: here we'll explore the physiological truths about this art, including such concepts as resonance, support, breath, vibrato, intonation, and dynamics. You'll learn an efficient and reliable vocal technique that should help you find your true sound in any style or context. Finally, we'll combine the two into an approach that will help you transcend the challenges of performing in song. *This* is the living DNA strand, the "code" for creating outstanding performances that will be beautiful, unique, and authentically yours.

# ACKNOWLEDGMENTS

There are far too many people to thank for the help they gave me in writing this book. Countless talented and generous people have crossed my path and taught me something, even if they weren't conscious of it. That said, the following souls deserve special recognition.

To my beautiful wife, Nicole: your unrelenting love, support, and belief in me is the greatest gift I could ever wish for. We've shared so much, and I can't wait for our next adventures together!

To my mom, Sue: you always encouraged me to pursue my dreams and have been there for me every single day of my life. I'm so proud of you—and your writing, too!

To my children, Garrison and Geneva: you are my living miracles. You've brought so much joy and purpose to the lives of your grateful parents. You are wonderful, amazing, and we couldn't be prouder.

To Bill Connington: you, sir, are a true gentleman and first-class colleague. Your generosity and encouragement made this book possible. And your effortless talent and depth of character set the best example for all of us to follow.

To my agent, Barbara Clark: you are simply the best. As a first-time author, I was truly a lost little lamb in the woods without you. You have been a rock and a ray of sunshine for me. I cannot imagine a better agent, editor, and advocate for my work.

To Jennifer Aylmer: thank you so much for your generosity in sharing your unmatched knowledge of both vocal pedagogy and artistic expression with me. Some of the strongest core beliefs and concepts in this book I learned from you.

To Frank Lopardo: you are my friend, my colleague and my Maestro. Boy am I lucky to have one of the greatest tenors of all-time as my teacher. We are just getting started!

To performing artists everywhere: may you continue to practice resiliency with an unrelenting belief in your talent. I wish you continued strength and encouragement. Dream the most audacious dreams and forge a path to reach them!

# INTRODUCTION

I'm beyond excited to share with you what I've come to believe are the simple, basic truths of singing and acting. One of these truths concerns technique: great technique should be virtually invisible. Technique is the undetectable story delivery system, the system we employ when we need to get out of our own way. Think of watching great athletes compete at the Olympics. When Usain Bolt is setting world records, he has a huge smile across his face. Great divers plunge into water from ten meters and barely make a splash. This is because they have superior technique, which allows their bodies to work efficiently under pressure. It's the same thing with great singing and acting. Meryl Streep transforms so completely that she makes acting look easy. Luciano Pavarotti appeared so relaxed on stage that it seemed as if he were enjoying a back massage. This is what I aim to help you experience for yourself: a *free* voice. Which voice? Why, all of them—your singing voice *and* your true acting voice.

First I'd like to share with you a bit of my story. I came to performing toward the end of high school (on a dare from my mother) and found myself cast in a Second World War musical called *Over Here*. I don't remember much about it other than that I had to come up with a "Joysee" (i.e., New Jersey) accent with the help of a cast member's mother who grew up in the Garden State. I also remember feeling incredibly self-conscious. From there, my grandfather helped me gain acceptance to the Interlochen National Music Camp (now known as the Interlochen International Arts Center). I think he was motivated to keep me away from his summer cottage (where I tended to carouse with college students), and the two-month-long program was the perfect way to do it. I reluctantly agreed to go. To say it was a life-changing experience would be an understatement. It was there that I learned I was a tenor (albeit a very bad one in the beginning). I also discovered that I could sing sustained high notes with relative ease. For me, this was the equivalent of being able to dunk a basketball while jumping over a car. The rest of my voice was a mess, and my vibrato sounded like an erratic machine gun. Nevertheless, I was determined to explore my newfound ability, and I began taking formal voice lessons.

My voice was still plagued by that erratic vibrato, but I began learning art songs and Italian repertoire. Then I managed to get a few modest scholarship offers to study voice at several Midwestern universities. I eventually chose Miami University, in Oxford, Ohio. There I studied under a patient, talented, and energetic tenor named Clayton Parr. Within the first three months of my training, my voice suddenly "popped open" like kernels of corn. I could sing with a consistent tone and an even vibrato. Although I knew next to nothing about acting, at this point I knew I could really sing. Miami gave me numerous opportunities to sing and perform, and there I developed my confidence and a degree of comfort on stage. I also grew much more ambitious with what I wanted to do with my singing, so I transferred to the University of Michigan's prestigious musical theater program.

During my time in Ann Arbor, I went from knowing virtually nothing about musical theater to becoming a full-fledged Broadway geek. I also met another great voice teacher, George Shirley, a pioneer and personal hero of mine. A Grammy-nominated singer, he is the first African American tenor to perform leading roles at the Metropolitan Opera. In training me, he was tough, funny, and encouraging. Even though I was majoring in musical theater, he encouraged me to continue my classical training. I even spent a summer at the Aspen Music Festival and School, where he was on the faculty, so I could continue my training with him.

This oscillating between singing and acting has been a constant in my training and professional career. For many years, I felt that I had to choose one over the other, which led to much confusion and soul-searching. Upon graduation from Michigan, I chose to focus on acting and moved to New York City. My first job qualified me to join the Actors' Equity Association, and I worked in several regional and Off-Broadway theaters over the following three years. Unfortunately, something big was missing in my audition process, and that was a consistent, reliable acting technique. Even though I already had a BFA (a degree that confers zero guarantees of future employment), it became clear to me that I needed to immerse myself in acting training outside the context of singing. At that time, my singing was basically how I defined myself, so taking it away was a scary push outside my comfort zone.

That said, the three years I spent at the University of Washington's Professional Actor Training Program were the most important years of my life as a developing artist. At the UW School of Drama, my course work included speech training, immersion in the Alexander Technique, and the study of Shakespeare, scansion, and script analysis. All this gave me a strong foundation in acting as well as the skills necessary to be a successful stage actor. In addition, it was at UW that I became a teaching assistant, teaching introduction to acting to undergraduates. This was another discovery—I found I had a voice within the art form of storytelling.

Upon graduation, Adam Guettel and Craig Lucas cast me in the first professional production of *The Light in the Piazza*. I performed in the show at the Intiman and Goodman Theatres, originating the role of Giuseppe, and continued as an understudy and swing in the Broadway production at the Lincoln Center Theater. My involvement with Piazza put me in the room with some of the most talented and influential people in the field of musical theater, including Kelli O'Hara, Victoria Clark, Bartlett Sher, Ted Sperling, and Matthew Morrison. Artistically, this is about as close to heaven as it gets for a singing actor. Fully dramatically integrated new musicals are rare on Broadway, and I felt that I was part of something that was historically important.

*Piazza*, with its soaring score and many Italian lyrics, also opened my mind to the possibility of singing operatically. While working on the Lincoln Center campus, I would occasionally run into colleagues from my undergraduate days at the University of Michigan. One of them happened to be a young man, Howard Watkins, who had risen to become a coach and associate conductor at the Metropolitan Opera. He introduced me to one of the top vocal teachers in the field of opera, and I was suddenly dreaming of singing opera professionally. Five years of blood, sweat, and tears later, I was represented by a respected manager of classical singers and being paid to sing opera! Since that time, I've performed more than twenty operas while continuing to work steadily as an actor. In the meantime, I've built a strong private teaching practice and am now in my fifth year as a member of the acting faculty at the Yale School of Drama.

I tell you all this to paint a picture of the nonlinear path that brought me to this point in my career. At times it has been messy, painful, and confusing, but it has also rewarded me with countless beautiful moments. Above all, I've learned a tremendous amount about the art of living through song, and I continue to be as fascinated by it as I was twenty-five years ago.

I wish you success on your journey.

# 1
# THE SINGER ACTS

We begin with acting because, first and foremost, performers are storytellers. Without story, singing would just be a jumble of (potentially) pretty sounds without any context. This kind of performance is almost certain to repel an audience. After all, singing is what we do when speech is no longer adequate to express what we want to say. It's a heightened way of telling a story.

## What is acting?

But what is acting? Acting is a very simple thing that we tend to overcomplicate. When some people try to act, their behavior resembles that of a space alien or robot attempting to mimic human activity. This is because they are focusing on what they think acting is supposed to look like instead of on what they are doing—on what the character *wants*. When I forget this on stage, I feel like I'm standing behind my body and manipulating it as if it were a puppet. Sound familiar?

By definition, acting is living truthfully in imaginary circumstances. Every one of us has used our imaginations, and every one of us has been a child, so we can understand that acting is really like playing a game of make-believe. If you've sometimes felt painfully self-conscious while acting, as I have, it's probably because you're focusing on the wrong things. You are focusing on yourself instead of on where you are, whom you are talking to, what you want, and how you plan to get it—the imaginary circumstances.

Acting while singing should be no less truthful than any other style of acting. The biggest difference between spoken acting and sung acting is that in addition to the imaginary circumstances of a scene—setting, situation, personal relationships—songs give us further given circumstances that must be taken into account. Given circumstances (see page 14) are facts that are either explicit (stated in the text) or implicit (implied). In singing, the most obvious given circumstance is pitch—the notes, the melody—usually accompanied by instrumentation, which partners with the given circumstances in the text.

## Acting and belief

My journey into acting training started by the simple desire to know what to do with my hands. During performances, I felt almost immobile, like an inanimate object. A lot of personal insecurities and deeply held belief systems came into play. I used to think that the talent gods had blessed some actors, but they hadn't blessed me. I put the idea of acting on a pedestal: I worshipped it as if it were some mystical gift that I might occasionally receive. What I didn't yet know was that acting is an art form that can be approached as a science. Many great actors and teachers have been exploring and documenting this science for centuries. So if you believe you have no acting talent, you're right! You are what you think, so this is the first problem you'll need to address. This belief system, which is held deeply in your subconscious, will sabotage you at every turn. You need to begin telling yourself positive facts, such as:

"I am as unique as my fingerprints, and there is no one else in the world like me."
"I have an actor's voice, and I will be heard!"
"I just need technique, training, and experience to set my actor free."

The vast majority of actors have worked incredibly hard to develop as artists. Acting is a craft that must be practiced and refined, which allows us to slowly eliminate bad habits and personal obstacles from our work. Successful performers possess grit and vision: they stick with it and grow when they encounter failure. They embrace these failures as part of the learning process. So if you believe that there's an actor inside you, buried deeply or close to the surface, you're right!

## Song selection

The first step in learning to approach singing as an act of storytelling is to choose a song to work on. This isn't as easy as it sounds! You may have favorite styles of singing or genres of music, and you may have certain examples of them running through your head. Maybe there's a particular performance of a song that inspires you. But at this stage I'm going to ask you to put all that aside so that you don't end up imitating a particular performance. Choose a song that has a strong message, preferably one that is sung *to* someone—a partner on or off stage. I encourage you to always think of anything you do on stage as a scene between you and someone else.

Approach the song as a theatrical *scene.* As an example, consider "If I Loved You," sung by the character Billy Bigelow in Rodgers and Hammerstein's musical *Carousel*. This song is part of a larger scene, usually referred to as the bench scene, between Billy and his beloved, the character Julie Jordan. I'm fond of this song because it's been described as a *conditional love song*. Although he is clearly in love with Julie, Billy never actually says "I love you." Below are the lyrics:

> If I loved you, time and again I would try to say all I'd want you to know.
> If I loved you, words wouldn't come in an easy way. Round in circles I'd go.
> Longing to tell you, but afraid and shy,
> I'd let my golden chances pass me by.
> Soon, you'd leave me. Off you would go in the midst of day.
> Never, never to know how I loved you.
> If I loved you.

This song has been sung by many brilliant performers over the years. In the first production, Billy Bigelow was played by John Raitt. His interpretation still might be the best, in my opinion, because Mr. Raitt combined his shimmering and virile vocals with an honest and vulnerable characterization. In the Lincoln Center revival of *Carousel*, Michael Hayden played Billy with a nuance and danger not often seen in traditional musical theater. What he lacked in vocal power he more than made up for with his unpredictable and charismatic performance. Beyond the theater, "If I Loved You" has been interpreted by countless singers, including Frank Sinatra, Barbra Streisand, Julie Andrews, and Audra MacDonald. I encourage you to search online and view many different versions of the song. Decide which ones work for you and which ones don't, and write down your observations.

## EXERCISE 1: CHOOSE A SONG

- Choose a song or aria that you really like or want to work on. The style or genre is irrelevant, provided that it's been written for a character who feels and wants something very strongly. It will be easier for you to pick a piece from something theatrical (i.e., a musical or an opera), because most of the given circumstances are already determined.
- Find an empty notebook. On a blank page, handwrite the lyrics of your song. I feel that handwritten transcriptions help you absorb and process material more organically (and usually more quickly). When I'm preparing a new song, I always handwrite the lyrics first.
- If the lyrics are in a language you aren't fluent in, make sure to find an accurate translation. For operatic texts, I highly recommend using the translations of Nico Castel in his operatic libretti series. Most standard repertory operas have been translated in these volumes.
- Leave ample space to write between each sentence of the lyrics.
- Regarding punctuation, I prefer not to include it, with the exception of question marks. Punctuation can make us subconsciously see broken-up *phrases* in our head that may or may not translate to a larger *thought*. I find question marks useful, on the other hand, because they can actively put the onus back on your scene partner, which implies that you actively listen for his or her response.

# Telling the story

Telling a story through song involves breaking down the process into several smaller steps. Each of these steps—finding the action, finding the obstacle, finding the beats, using tactics, recognizing the given circumstances, and setting the scene—allows us to internalize the momentum in a story, its forward progress, and allows us to most fully become the character who's singing.

## Finding the action

The *action* or *objective* of a song can be defined simply as what the singing character needs her scene partner to do, feel, or understand. In taking this step, it's important to find an action that feels specific, human, fun, and *active.*

Action is something we human beings do pretty much every minute of every day. We are always doing *something*, and it's always specific. Even when we're making our morning coffee, there are details to consider. How much time do we have to make the coffee? How much are we making? How do we make it—using a grinder, an automatic drip machine, a Keurig? Are we trying not to wake others in the house? Why do we want the coffee? Did we get a bad night's sleep? Do we have a stressful day ahead of us? Think about your day *right now.* What are you currently *doing?* Whatever it is, no matter how blasé it might seem, I guarantee it is a very specific *action.* Get in the habit of using strong, active verbs to describe what you're doing.

In "If I Loved You," Billy Bigelow is in a situation that makes him uncomfortable. He's on a date with a seemingly naive young woman, expecting a little hanky-panky. Instead he finds himself having deep romantic feelings for her, but he doesn't quite know how to confess these feelings. How could we find an action to play as Billy Bigelow in this scene? Beginning with an active verb, I'll go with *declare*. "Declare" is a good, strong word, but it's not specific enough for me to play. I'll translate it to "open my heart to her," which feels playable. I say "playable" because it's vital that we think of our actions as play, as a game of make-believe. To *confess* or *confide* could be other active verb choices. In this case I could play "get this weight off of my shoulders" or "exhale my truth."

## EXERCISE 2: FIND THE ACTION

- In your notebook, next to the lyrics of your song, make a list of ten active verbs, such as *penetrate, enlighten, instruct, dazzle,* and *intimidate*, that seem appropriate for the action of the song.
- Now, this is a good start, but these verbs are just the entry point. From them, you have to find a *playable* action. So let's make things more human and fun. This means finding equivalent phrases—including idioms—that activate *you* and the way you relate to language colloquially and informally.
- Think of idiomatic expressions that can be substituted for each of your ten verbs. For example, for the verb *penetrate*, you could say "get it through his thick skull." For *enlighten*, how about "show her the light"? See where I'm going with this?
- Looking at your song (which I'd prefer you to think of as a scene), decide whom you are talking to. Is it the audience? Is it one person? Is it a group of people? Is it yourself?
- Once you have determined this, make a decision about what you *need* from that person or people. Make sure you choose something active.
- Decide how you are going to get what you need from whomever you're talking to, then translate that verb into an idiomatic expression. Write it down and ask yourself if it sounds like something you'd like to *play.*
- If it feels too clinical—for example, "get the information"—find something more colloquial, such as "make him sing like a canary" or "butter her up."
- Make a list of at least three actions you relate to in your gut, not just your brain, and try them out. Which one feels right? Which one seems the easiest to *commit* to? (Hint: the action should be something that doesn't make you feel self-conscious.)

## Finding the obstacles

An obstacle is an impediment that blocks you from performing your action and getting what you want. It is also what helps you to be specific about your action and the tactics you use to accomplish your goal. Obstacles create *conflict,* and conflict creates *drama*. Billy Bigelow, for example, is a character who is fairly rough and likes to be in control. It's also suggested that he was abused as a child, so vulnerability is not something he wants to feel. That being said, he doesn't chase Julie away, so he clearly wants to be there with her.

So what's the obstacle? Is it that she already has told him that she has feelings for him? Is it that he is torn between wanting to simply hook up with her on the one hand and wanting to consider her as something more, as a potential wife, on the other? Is it his fear of intimacy, which he finds painful and uncomfortable? Notice that not all obstacles come from outside the character. Some of the obstacles are clearly *internal*. All the obstacles stand in conflict with Billy's action, which is that he's trying to tell her he's falling in love with her. To state these obstacles in a playable fashion, he might say, "She'll make my heart bleed," "This isn't what I signed up for," or "No one gets close to me."

Imagine that you are viewing this scene as a close-up camera shot of the entire play. What would happen if you zoomed out and looked at

### EXERCISE 3: FIND THE OBSTACLES

- **Using the action you liked best from the last part of Exercise 2, try to find an obstacle in your song that's equally strong. If it's not strong enough, it won't work, because you'll have nothing to fight against (hence, no drama). What you need to find is the most extreme push-pull scenario. When the action and obstacle are well matched, it's as if you are *literally* pushing against something that is incredibly strong. Your action and obstacle should be like a clash of Titans!**
- **Find at least five obstacles and write them in your notebook.**

the play as a whole? From this point of view, I'd like you to decide what you think the overall story is about—what's the action of the entire play? And what's the obstacle? Look at other scenes for clues and ideas. In *Carousel*, one might say it's a play about risking everything, including your life, for love. The greatest obstacle in the play could be *time*. There's never enough time to spend with your loved ones, and the historical time period could be cruel, especially to the poor and underprivileged.

## Finding the beats

Every scene should have several events, decisions, or discoveries that alter the way we pursue our goals. These events are also known as beats. They can be internal or external. An internal beat might occur at the point when you (as the character) realize that you are not feeling safe with the other character. Maybe you are giddily singing about love and happiness to a character who's in mourning for a loved one, so you adjust your giddiness to something more sober. Perhaps there's a musical shift or cue that feels foreboding. An external beat can occur because of something your scene partner does—perhaps she turns her back on you or starts to walk away. Or maybe a phone rings. I generally prefer to find four beats, including one that occurs at the top of the scene, before the music starts, in every scene or song I play. This keeps variety in the story, which in turn keeps things interesting and unpredictable.

Let's look at two potential beats or beat shifts in "If I Loved You." Immediately before the song, Julie says, "But you don't [love me], right?" to which Billy replies, "No, I don't!" He then proceeds to sing the introductory section of the song, which contains the lyrics "But somehow I can see just exactly how I'd be." So what makes him deny his feelings for Julie, then do an about-face on his next breath? *This* is a clear beat shift that needs to be explored.

First, *why* does he say that he doesn't love Julie? What action was he playing? Let's say his action was something like "Okay, kid, I'll play along," but he realizes that she's taking everything seriously. This compels his "No, I don't!" response. Here he could be really saying "Let's not get carried away!" This would be a clear, playable beat shift. He immediately shifts his position again, saying, "But somehow I can see just exactly how I'd be." What could've happened to make him adjust so quickly? Perhaps he sees something in Julie's eyes that melts his heart. Maybe Julie begins to tremble and cry.

### EXERCISE 4: FIND THE BEATS

- **In your notebook, divide the text of your scene or song into four sections, each preceded by a beat.**
- **Give each beat a name by identifying or deciding what your scene partner says or does before the beat.**
- **Determine how each beat changes, removes, or adds an obstacle to your action.**

## Using tactics

Now that you've identified four beats in your song or scene, and now that you've discovered how the obstacles change (or increase or decrease) as a result, you will need to adjust your strategy for overcoming the obstacles accordingly. These strategies are called *tactics*. You need to change them because whatever you're using is no longer working after the obstacle shift. You can choose your tactics based on whatever you articulated as your action. For example, if in "If I Loved You" my action is "open my heart to Julie," how can I come up with an arsenal of tactics that will help me achieve my goal? By making a list of simple verbs:

- to persuade
- to reassure
- to warn
- to comfort
- to surrender
- to challenge
- to seduce
- to impress
- to evade

I can use these tactics at various points in the song, choosing a new tactic each time the beat changes and the obstacle shifts. One "tactic map" might look like this:

No, I don't! [Beat 1]
[Tactic 1: to soften]
But somehow I can see just exactly how I'd be
If I loved you, time and again I would try to say all I'd want you to know
If I loved you, words wouldn't come in an easy way. Round in circles I'd go [Beat 2]
[Tactic 2: to confess]
Longing to tell you, but afraid and shy,
I'd let my golden chances pass me by [Beat 3]
[Tactic 3: to threaten]
Soon you'd leave me
Off you would go in the midst of day
Never, never to know how I loved you [Beat 4]
[Tactic 4: to recover]
If I loved you.

## EXERCISE 5: USE TACTICS

- **Draw up a list of seven to ten tactics, expressed as a list of strong verbs. Make sure the list contains as much variety as possible.**
- **Create a map for your song, outlining the beats, the obstacles, and the strategies or tactics you plan to use to overcome them. Insert the appropriate verb whenever the beat changes.**
- **Make a second map for your song using a different set of tactics. Determine which works best; keep experimenting until you come up with the most effective plan.**

## Recognizing the given circumstances

Given circumstances are facts that we can gather from the text that help us make specific decisions about playing a scene. We can separate given circumstances into the categories of explicit and implicit. Explicit circumstances can include where the scene takes place, whether it's indoors or outdoors, the time of day, the historical period, and biographical facts about the character, such as age, education level, profession, and so on.

Regarding "If I Loved You," some of the explicit given circumstances are as follows:

- The action takes place on a beach in Maine on a moonlit night in June.
- Billy Bigelow is an itinerant carnival barker, which means he won't be in town long.
- Julie Jordan works at a mill in town, is a teenager, and resides in a girl's dormitory that enforces strict rules and a curfew, which she's violating.
- The action takes place in 1873.

Implicit given circumstances are not stated in the text and are therefore open to interpretation. We may use them at our discretion, but we must be careful to ensure they are reasonable assumptions or deductions that adhere closely to the explicit given circumstances. The implicit circumstances are those that sometimes provide the best ammunition for specific acting opportunities and can really add juice and higher stakes to the scene. Continuing with "If I Loved You," what else can we possibly assume?

- Neither character has much (if any) formal education.
- Both characters might be orphans.
- Billy could be a victim of physical (or sexual) abuse.
- Neither character has any money saved, meaning that losing their jobs would be very risky.
- Julie is a virgin.

Departing from *Carousel,* let's consider another example, this time from the dramatic literature of William Shakespeare. Performing Shakespeare shares many challenges with performing a song in that both are written in *heightened* language that needs to be expressed *truthfully.* In a scene from Shakespeare's *Macbeth,* the character of Macduff learns that his wife and children have been slaughtered. It would be fairly safe to assume that Macduff is incredibly upset when he hears this information. How could we use this to our advantage in playing Macduff?

First I'll map out some *explicit* circumstances about this scene.

- Macduff is the Thane of Fife, in medieval Scotland. A thane is a royal official, similar to an earl. This is the same rank as Macbeth.
- Macduff is the one who discovers the corpse of King Duncan.
- Macduff suspects, accurately, that Macbeth is guilty of regicide (the murder of King Duncan).
- Macduff is a husband and a father.
- Macduff is in London to raise an army against Macbeth.
- Macduff learns of his family's murder while informing Malcolm, Duncan's son, of his suspicions about Macbeth.
- Macduff learns of his family's murder from Ross, another thane.

Below is the text of the scene itself:

**MACDUFF**
All my pretty ones?
Did you say "all"? O hell-kite! All?
What, all my pretty chickens and their dam
At one fell swoop?

**MALCOLM**
Dispute it like a man.

**MACDUFF**
I shall do so,
But I must also feel it as a man.
I cannot but remember such things were
That were most precious to me. Did heaven look on
And would not take their part? Sinful Macduff,
They were all struck for thee! Naught that I am,

Not for their own demerits, but for mine,
Fell slaughter on their souls. Heaven rest them now.

**MALCOLM**
Be this the whetstone of your sword. Let grief
Convert to anger. Blunt not the heart; enrage it.

**MACDUFF**
O, I could play the woman with mine eyes
And braggart with my tongue! But, gentle heavens,
Cut short all intermission! Front to front
Bring thou this fiend of Scotland and myself.
Within my sword's length set him. If he 'scape,
Heaven forgive him too.

What *implicit* given circumstances can we determine from this scene?

- Macduff is enraged, heartbroken, devastated, shocked.
- Because he is in London, he is several days away from Scotland by horseback.
- He knew he was taking a risk in leaving his family behind in Scotland and lied about his official whereabouts while skipping Macbeth's coronation.
- If we judge him by his actions, Macduff is a man of honor with a strong moral code.
- Macduff is the polar opposite of Macbeth. He states that he must "feel it like a man": this is in contrast to Macbeth (and Lady Macbeth), who believe that real men deny their feelings.

How do we use these decisions to our advantage in *playing* this scene? We strive for variety from moment to moment so the audience doesn't simply see one tone or color in the character: this will lead them to tune out the performance because it's basically one-note. We always want to surprise the audience with our choices, provided they serve the story and character.

## EXERCISE 6: RECOGNIZE THE GIVEN CIRCUMSTANCES

- **Make a list of explicit and implicit given circumstances in your selected song. List ten explicit facts and ten implicit facts.**
- **Note what the exploration of these facts do to stimulate your imagination and desire to play the scene or song. Does it make your choices about how to play the character clearer?**

## Setting the scene

The setting of the scene is an extension of exploring the given circumstances. Simply put, *where are you* in the song? Be as specific as possible. Is it morning, afternoon, or evening? What time is it? Are you indoors or outdoors? What season is it? What's the weather like? Is it warm or cold? How warm? How cold? Are you in a public place? What's the view like? What year is it? How much time do you have? Could someone overhear your conversation? This is a part of acting that often gets overlooked, which means you're missing some real opportunities to play your action.

Let's think about one of my favorite songs, "Maria," sung by the character Tony in Bernstein and Sondheim's *West Side Story*. The explicit given circumstances of the song include the following facts:

- Tony is standing outside, at night, at approximately 10:00 or 11:00 p.m., following a dance.
- It's late spring or early summer and humid.
- Tony stands in an alley surrounded by fire escapes in a densely populated Puerto Rican neighborhood on the West Side of New York City.
- Tony is a former member of a street gang that maintained a fierce rivalry with a Puerto Rican street gang.
- Maria is Puerto Rican.
- It's approximately 1957.

Now let's think about the implicit given circumstances. These we can ponder by asking ourselves a series of questions.

- What would happen to Tony if he were overheard by any of his Puerto Rican enemies?
- Is Tony so intoxicated from meeting Maria that he is oblivious to his surroundings?
- Is Tony singing to a specific window and fire escape, or is he guessing and hoping that one of them belongs to Maria?
- How tall is the building that Tony stands in front of?
- What is Maria doing inside her apartment?

### EXERCISE 7: EXPLOIT YOUR SETTING

- **Write down the facts about the setting of your song. Are there any you can glean from the given circumstances explored in Exercise 6? Where does the scene take place geographically? Indoors? Outdoors? What time of day is it? What year? What's the temperature like?**
- **Look at what you have written and try to imagine that you're actually *in* the setting you chose. Try to imagine it in three dimensions.**
- **Speak the text of your song as if you were actually occupying the setting you've imagined in vivid detail.**
- **Do you feel that the specificity of setting helps you focus on another element that occurs *outside* your head?**

## The elevator pitch

An elevator pitch is a brief speech delivered by someone who has to convince someone else of something very important in the short time it takes for an elevator to travel between point A and point B. So obviously the pitch has to be really succinct, simple, and to the point.

Now that we've asked a lot of important questions about your song, I'd like you to tell me what the story is in *one sentence*. Elevator-pitch me. To describe "If I Loved You," for example, I could say it's a ballad about two people who would risk everything to be with each other despite having just met. To describe "Maria," I could say it's a love song about a young man discovering that he's come face to face with his destiny. This way of looking at your scene gives you a macroscopic vision of the story you're playing and will enable you to develop a vital skill: self-directing. Seeing the big picture allows you to take the pressure off yourself and put your focus on the story rather than on your own doubts and anxieties. It is your responsibility to *play* the scene, not *be* the scene.

### EXERCISE 8: WRITE AN ELEVATOR PITCH

- **Write down the story of your song, taking as much time as you'd like. Don't worry about how many sentences it takes.**
- **Imagine watching it as you've described it from the audience. Is it compelling? Is there something at stake? Is it too easy to predict what's going to happen?**
- **Write down the story of your song again, but only use one sentence. Again, does it seem compelling, with something at stake? If so, you've put together a *playable* elevator pitch.**

## Imagination

Have you ever read the children's book *Where the Wild Things Are* by Maurice Sendak? In it, a boy named Max gets sent to his room without dinner for misbehaving. He then imagines that his room literally turns into a sea, which he sails to a mysterious land where he encounters a jungle full of beasts. The journey begins with his bedposts becoming trees and his walls turning into vines, then his room disappears and he's actually transported. This is all attributable to the power and (in his case) the imperative of his imagination. He felt sad, cornered, and trapped, so he used his imagination to escape.

Interestingly, people come to the theater for the same reason—to escape. So as actors, it's our responsibility to be like Max: to employ our imaginations in a game of make-believe. This in turn awakens the audience's imagination! Beautiful, isn't it? In this chapter, we've done a lot of baseline work—asking questions about a scene, making decisions about many specific details concerning the setting and characters. Now it's time to put that work into action.

I've often heard people say that great actors actually believe they are the characters they play. Um … this is crazy. If that were true, actors would be clinically insane (not to mention extremely difficult to work with). In fact, what actors are tremendous at doing is *choosing* to be their characters and engaging in the *imagined* reality that they've chosen. It's up to you to always choose your imagined reality in a scene over the actual reality you are inhabiting, just as Max in *Where the Wild Things Are* does. If you are in an audition room, you have to decide and commit to the room transforming into another place—the place you've chosen to imagine!

In an era of smartphones, computers, and televisions, you're used to seeing images on a small screen. You'll be surprised how this has affected your ability to live in an imaginary world. Chances are you have flattened and miniaturized your imagery. Please take the opportunity to imagine things that include their actual size, shape, and depth. If you decide that you are in a forest, for example, make sure the trees are towering above you and not the size of your average Christmas tree. See the branches extending in whatever vivid colors you've chosen. The whole point of this is to help you escape the prison of your own self-consciousness.

## Physicality

Now that we've gotten your imagination stirring, you need to physicalize the concepts you've been studying. Having a thought process as a character will do you no good unless you can transmit it to the audience. We do this by activating the unique story-delivering machine called your body.

### The eyes

There never has been and never will be a great performance that doesn't begin with the eyes. In acting, as in poker, the eyes tell us everything. Have you ever struggled with being photographed? Do you feel uncomfortable in front of a camera? It probably begins with your eyes. You might be trying to show the camera that you're happy, so you put on a "smiley face." In those situations, you need to remember that acting is not about how you feel but what you want. So instead of trying to smile generically, try playing an action, such as "project an air of peace and joy." How did that change your eyes and face?

Many actors, myself included, can be overly concerned about what they are doing physically, especially in an audition. Unfortunately, this outside-in approach neglects the fact that you are playing a human being with a heart and soul. I recently spoke with a prominent Broadway casting director and asked him what was the biggest mistake actors consistently make in auditions. Without hesitation, he said, "There's all this physical activity and noise, some of it very slick and polished, but there's nothing behind their eyes." This really resonated with me because I've been guilty of this countless times. But it makes complete sense, doesn't it? After all, the eyes are windows to the soul.

## EXERCISE 9: BE AWARE OF YOUR EYES

- **Sit in a chair and look directly at something across the room. Observe the object in detail.**
- **Write down as many details as you can find, including the object's shape, size, color, texture, and age.**
- **Allow yourself to breathe and imagine the air gently flowing through your eyes as well as through your mouth and nose.**
- **How do your eyes *feel* when you do this?**
- **Find a blank wall space, stand up, and look directly at it from across the room.**
- **Imagine that the object you observed while sitting is hanging on the wall in that space. Decide the object is there and simply see it, the way you would if it were actually there.**
- **How do your eyes feel now? What's different and challenging? What other facial muscles try to engage? What changes do you perceive when you stare at something while you're standing up versus when you're sitting down?**

## Your face is a mask

Hey, you! Stop making faces! I'm sure you've heard this before, but *you are enough.* When acting, you are in the *action* business, not the *feeling* business. Again, it's never about how you feel as a character, but what you want.

As a human being with a life story singularly your own, you have to trust that a character's emotional life will read quite clearly and authentically through you if you simply commit to the action you are playing. You need to *make room* for your emotions, but if you try to *add* feelings to your performance, it will bleed into the scene and make it about an emotional *tone* instead of a *story.* The audience is looking for a dramatic performance, which means playing the conflict. If they sense that your performance is tonal, they will tune you out. For example, if your scene is about a breakup and you are simply crying and looking sad, the audience will read it as tonal and think, "Oh, it's about sadness." Wouldn't you rather have the audience read it as dramatic and think something like, "Oh, my God, she must be devastated. How is she going to handle this?"

This all comes back to the eyes and face. Your face is the canvas onto which the audience projects its own imaginations and feelings. Earlier, I mentioned that I sometimes felt like I was manipulating my own puppet when acting. What I didn't understand is that an actor is basically a *living* puppet. Therefore, I *am* the puppet. Puppets fascinate me because of the variety of emotions they seem to project with little to no change of expression in their eyes or faces. Think of Kermit—can he blink? Do his eyes move? Does he have eyebrows and a forehead? No: he's manipulated by a master puppeteer who makes the most of his character's extremely limited facial mobility. And what's the result? To me, Kermit is an extremely sensitive character, capable of projecting joy, sadness, sweetness, kindness, and, occasionally, hysterically funny frenetic energy. This is because *I'm* projecting these emotional states onto *him*.

So what can we learn from Kermit about ourselves in performance? Among other things, that we all have many physical habits that bleed into our performances. If we gently build an awareness of them, we can begin to remove them from our acting process. We need to think of the writers (or the composers and lyricists) as the master puppeteers and our unaffected selves as the puppets. We need to trust that we are *enough.*

### EXERCISE 10: BE AWARE OF YOUR FACE

- **Put two strips of Scotch tape vertically on your forehead, between the tops of your eyebrows and your hairline.**
- **Speak the text of your song, with intention, to your imaginary scene partner.**
- **What did you notice about your forehead and eyebrows? Did they move a lot? Did any of your facial muscles engage that you didn't intend or choose to engage?**

## Go to the zero

Something we rarely take into account is the fact that the simple act of walking on stage is interesting to an audience. They've come to the theater to escape, not to judge you. They are looking to get lost in a story and are going to project the story onto you. Therefore, it is your job to make your problems the *character's* problems. If you are nervous, allow the character to be nervous, and fight as the character would to stay calm.

Now, there are going to be many times in auditioning and performing when you might feel lost, insecure, unfocused, or self-conscious. This is likely because you haven't been specific about a particular moment or scene. When this happens, actors often panic and decide that they have to *do* something—gesturing, moving, making a face. I strongly suggest in these moments that you remember you are interesting when doing nothing. A living, breathing human being automatically captures the attention of an audience. This moment of panic is the time to *go to the zero.*

This means that you should be as *simple* as possible. Don't try to *indicate* what you think the character is feeling. Simply soften your eyes, breathe, let go of any physical or emotional tension you may be feeling, and recommit to the person or persons you are talking to. Is it an imaginary scene partner? Is it the audience? Is it another actor sharing the stage with you? Be as specific as possible and stay simple until you feel focused on something other than yourself.

It's as if you are in a film and the camera is taking a close-up of your face. The camera detects even the slightest amount of tension, so just do nothing. Try playing several simple scenarios that would justify being fully engaged and present without any movement. This should keep you physically activated but also incredibly still, like a powerful car with its engine on but idling in neutral. Go to the zero!

### EXERCISE 11: GO TO THE ZERO

- **Imagine that a terrifying monster (maybe a T. rex) is circling you, looking for you, but he can only detect movement and therefore can't see you unless you stir. At any moment he could possibly smell or sense you, so you'd have to be ready to run for your life.**
- **Decide to move as quickly and quietly to another place in the room, then resume being actively still.**
- **How did this feel? Can you sense the potential energy and explosiveness in your body?**
- **Repeat, dashing quickly to another place in the room. Sense that even in stillness, *anything* is physically possible. This is a way to keep yourself available to spontaneous physical impulses and active beat shifts when performing.**

## Three circles

Imagine two circles sitting side by side. We'll name the circle on the left *underplay* and the circle on the right *overplay*. Now let's imagine a third circle placed between the two original circles, overlapping both of them—a kind of Venn diagram (Figure 1). This circle thus includes qualities of underplay and overplay but also has a surface area all to itself. Let's call this circle *interplay*.

The majority of the time, we should strive to live in this third circle. This is not to say that we can't engage in moments of stillness or moments of explosivity—these are valuable tools that add variety to our performances and depth and range to our characterizations. However, the ideal place to be is in an active state that has the potential to go in any direction. This is the physical state of readiness when you live within a problem.

Think of a shortstop in baseball when a pitch is thrown. Coiled like a snake ready to strike, he's leaning forward with his knees bent at the ready. Or a ballerina at the moment before she demonstrates a triple pirouette. She's in a long, deep plié, ready to leap to her toes and spin elegance and power. The athlete and the dancer are both living in the third circle—interplay.

When we examine the first circle, underplay, we need to differentiate between relaxation and activation. To be honest, as an actor, I don't find the word "relaxation" useful. Nothing about that word implies living in the fight of a scene. Acting is not casual, and we shouldn't think of having a physical off switch. A more useful word might be "stillness." So if you're looking for a quiet moment in a performance (perhaps your character is in shock, contemplative, or giving another character the "silent treatment"), remember to keep the potential for movement—an active state of readiness—alive in your body. There is still breath and blood moving through your system; your heart is beating, and you are completely aware of your surroundings. You'll never need an off switch because even your quietest moments are active.

If you're occupying the third circle, overplay, you're probably playing an action that isn't tempered by a strong obstacle. For example, if you find yourself yelling at your scene partner for any length of time, it would be highly improbable that you'd be able to achieve your objective—i.e.,

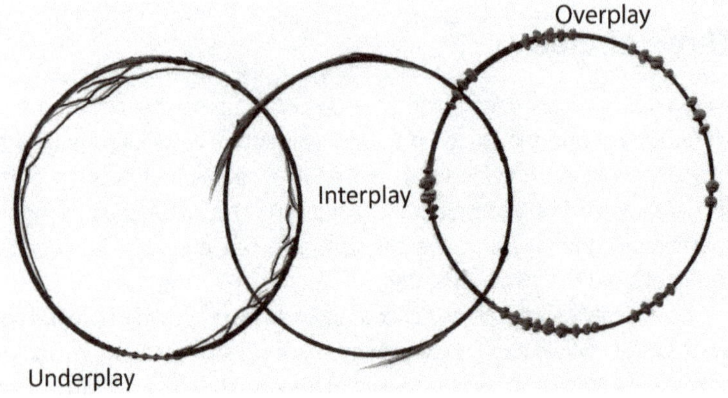


**Figure 1** Three circles.

convince her of anything or persuade her to do something. The same is true if you find yourself waving your fists and making unfocused physical gesticulations.

## EXERCISE 12: OBSERVE AND DESCRIBE

- Think of a performance that you found off-putting because it was forced and overdone. Think of an actor who seems to have become a *caricature* rather than a character. Have you often felt yourself pushing like this on stage or in auditions?
- Write down in detail what you dislike about this actor or performance. Describe these qualities using at least five adjectives.
- Describe, using verbs, what the actor is doing *physically.*
- Think of a stage performer whom you really admire. What is it about him or her that you find appealing? Can you recall a specific performance that made a positive impression on you?
- Write down in detail what you like about this actor or performance. Describe these qualities using at least five adjectives.
- Describe, using verbs, what the actor is doing *physically.*
- Imagine yourself being in the same physical state, with the potential for anything to happen at any time.

## EXERCISE 13: FIND THE THIRD CIRCLE

- Identify the final beat in your scene or song.
- Speak the text as loudly as possible.
- Say it again, but this time use your entire body and match your physical intensity to your vocal intensity.
- Note how this exercise makes you feel in your body. Are you tighter and more constricted? Or do you sense physical ease and expansion? I feel physically diminished, in spite of my attempts to become "bigger," when I do this exercise.

## Opposites

I like to think of everything I do on stage as having a strong push–pull relationship, like the relationship between actions and obstacles. Another way to say this is that I like to play *opposites.* Without an oppositional force, we can simply find ourselves flailing away on stage. Think of the law of gravity. Gravity is what keeps us from floating away into space and keeps us grounded. It's also a constant force that we continuously fight every waking day of our lives. We spend our first year in this world learning how to stand and walk against it, then run and leap. But no matter how high we jump, we come back down, because gravity always wins. It's an ever-present, undeniable force. This is a perfect metaphor for the concept of opposites we should employ in our acting.

### EXERCISE 14: PLAY THE OPPOSITES

- Think of an emotion (happiness, fear, sadness).
- Think of a manifestation of that emotion (laughing, trembling, weeping).
- Purposely try to play that emotion for one minute by performing its physical manifestation.
- How did that feel? Was there anywhere to go with it? Was there variety? Was there a story?
- Now play it again, but this time try to do the opposite. Try *not* to laugh; try *not* to tremble; try *not* to weep.
- How did that feel? Was there anywhere to go with it? Was there variety? Was there a story?
- The second attempt is based in action. More important, it's based in human behavior, which is more *active* and interesting. It gave you something to fight and *play*. And it included a story: "Will she cry? What is she feeling?"

## Breath, thought, and feelings

Your breath is literally your life. We survive by inhaling oxygen every minute of every day. Oxygen feeds every part of our bodies, including our brains, where thoughts originate. If you are trying to act and don't have a thought process, you might as well save us all a lot of pain and simply walk off the stage.

When we breathe and think, we take in our scene partners and our surroundings, and we constantly adjust our tactics for achieving our objectives. Try to think right now: what did you have for breakfast this morning? Now tell me: did you inhale before you could think? This is exactly what you should be doing as an actor. Don't hold your breath and say your lines—breathe before you speak. If you really know what the scene is about, you never have to predetermine *how* to say your lines. You have to trust yourself and your talent in these moments. Breathe, and you'll find that you'll *always* be authentic.

Many actors neglect to breathe freely, which blocks their ability to discover what's happening in the scene on a moment-to-moment basis. This might seem obvious, but acting can often feel extremely uncomfortable. This discomfort can include fear, nervousness, anxiety, insecurity, and many other negative feelings. If we don't breathe, we don't have to *feel*. If this sounds familiar to you, I suggest you start to embrace and acknowledge everything you feel, both on and off stage. Feelings are often illogical and out of proportion with an event, but still need to be given room to run their course. A great way to deal with feelings is to make them the *character's* problem. Incorporate them into whatever you're playing, and the audience will assume it's part of the scene. Make room for the feelings and fight for what you want, always putting your action first.

### EXERCISE 15: BREATHE BEFORE SPEAKING

- **Write a line of text that your scene partner might say before the first line of your song.**
- **Imagine your partner speaking the line. (This exercise is even more effective if you can find a friend who will speak**

**the other line in person so you don't have to imagine the exchange.)**

- **Inhale, then speak your first line. Make sure you don't predetermine how you are going to say it.**
- **Repeat, but this time imagine your scene partner saying his or her line with a different intention.**
- **Inhale, then speak your first line again, allowing your intention to be different in response to your partner's.**

## Target, intention, and truth

It is vital that you understand that *nothing* about acting is realistic. You don't walk down the street having spontaneous conversations in song. It's not realistic to be standing on a set in front of a group of people, wearing a costume and makeup and pretending that you aren't enacting a story that's already been written. What will make your performance truthful and potentially transcendent is a result of how deeply invested you are in playing *make-believe*, in creating truth out of imaginary circumstances. From the audience's perspective, there may seem to be elements of realism or naturalism in your performance. But your focus and commitment should always be on your *actions*. Remember that it's always about *what* you are doing, not *how well* you are doing it. The "How well am I doing?" voice will keep you stuck in the analytical part of your brain, making it nearly impossible for you to experience the trust, freedom, and joy of letting go.

This brings us to the issues of *target* and *intention*. By this point you have taken very clear steps to determine who your scene partner is. This person is your primary *target*. Every physical and vocal gesture you make is for him or her. When you are using tactics to execute your action, make sure the tactics are *landing* on your scene partner. This gives you a concrete purpose, which takes the mental focus off yourself.

There is always another scene partner you must take into consideration: the audience. Some actors try to bring their performance *to* the audience, but this is a mistake. This forced energy will have the effect of reminding them that you are Acting with a capital *A*. Remember, the audience came to the theater to escape. Help them suspend disbelief and invest in the story you are telling.

The best approach for a stage-worthy performance is to act with *intention*. Your performance must include something visible and audible for each and every member of the audience, including the folks in the last row. Now, you can't literally play to the entire house in every moment, so how do you accomplish this? Think of aiming toward your primary target but including the audience in your periphery. They are your ever-present secondary target (after all, you are performing for their benefit). Make sure you always *invite* them into your performance, and the result will be generous, truthful, and appropriate in size to whatever space you are playing in and whatever audience you are playing for.

## EXERCISE 16: INVITE THE AUDIENCE IN

- **Picture in your mind three distinctly different performance spaces that you've either performed in or attended a performance in. Think of them ranging from small to large. Choose spaces that greatly contrast with each other in size, shape, and seating capacity. Perhaps one space is an audition room, another a small black-box theater, and the third a vast auditorium capable of seating thousands.**
- **Once you have selected the three spaces, write down as many details about them as possible. How large or small is each space? Is the audience spread out horizontally or is the theater narrow? Is there a balcony? Is the stage a standard proscenium arch or a thrust? Can you remember what the space smells like? (Scent is a powerful tool in sensory recall.) What color is the space? Write as many details as you can remember. If you don't remember many details, make some up and imagine what it looks like.**
- **Imagine yourself standing center stage facing your scene partner, standing parallel to you. As you picture this, make sure your body**

and head are cheating out a bit so that most of your face and body can be seen by your scene partner *and* the audience. Make sure you can imagine yourself doing this in all three spaces.

- How do the differences among the spaces change the way you think you'd feel and relate to the audience?
- If possible, find an empty rehearsal room or a large space where you can be undisturbed. Otherwise, simply stand up in the room you are currently occupying.
- Decide that you are in the smallest space you chose and act out the text of your song as a scene with your imaginary partner. Include beat shifts that change your physical relationship with your partner *and* the audience. Make sure that everything you do vocally and physically is in appropriate size and proportion to your imagined space and audience.
- How did this feel to you? Could you trust that you were doing enough physically without pushing or growing your gestures and expressions? Would you have been heard by everyone?
- Act out the text of your song again, imagining yourself in the medium-size space, then the largest space.
- How did this affect your physical and vocal energy? Were you able to commit without feeling self-conscious?
- Try this at least five times for each imagined space. The repetition will increase your comfort and trust in your ability to truthfully adjust your performance to any specific space and audience.

# 2
# THE ACTOR SINGS

Think for a moment about your favorite singers. What is it about them that you respond to? Is it their vocal range? Their high notes? The beauty of their sound? My favorite singers have a sound so unique that I can identify them within seconds of hearing them. In my own singing, my goal is to get out of my own way, physically and mentally, so that I can consistently produce my fullest, freest, and most authentic sound.

How does all this apply to you? For starters, you don't need a polished and highly trained voice to have a singing career. Some of the most famous singers in history could barely sing a note. Think of Bob Dylan, Louis Armstrong, and Tom Waits. Mabel Mercer couldn't really carry a tune but is widely considered one of the greatest cabaret performers of all time. And nonsingers such as Rex Harrison, Yul Brynner, and the indomitable Elaine Stritch (fondly referred to by many as Elaine Screech) have delivered iconic Broadway performances. This isn't to suggest that you can't or shouldn't develop a strong, reliable vocal technique. I'm just pointing out that there's always a place for great storytellers in the world of song. So if you have little to no confidence in your singing ability, just remember that without a desire to communicate, singing is just an exercise in making empty sounds.

## What is singing?

What is singing, exactly? Let's find a definition that feels both specific and primal. Singing is what we *must* do when spoken text is simply inadequate to express what we want. We are compelled to sing, to release something *greater* than mere words.

Singing is *primal* in that it's related to crying, wailing, laughing, warning, threatening, and screaming. As a human being, you must remember that you are an animal. Can you think of an animal that doesn't have the ability to phonate (make sound)? Almost all animals make sound as a crucial component of their fight for survival. Early humans (those with limited or no formal language at their disposal), too, successfully used their voices to communicate and defend themselves. Like other animals, I imagine they growled, grunted, roared, whimpered, screamed, and cried in place of speaking.

In addition, singing is highly *specific* because it involves predetermined pitches (musical notes), rhythm, and text (lyrics). Combine these two elements, the *primal* and the *specific*, and voilà: you have singing.

When we are born into this world, we are naked, tiny, and completely helpless. We cannot see, walk, stay warm, or feed ourselves—everything we perceive as a baby feels like a life-or-death situation. From the point of view of a fragile and vulnerable animal (which is what a baby is), it's alone in the wilderness whenever a parent leaves it alone in its crib. So vocally, a baby's phonation is made when the stakes are at their highest possible level: it is crying for its very survival.

Have you ever marveled at the sheer volume of a baby's wailing? And does a baby ever seem to lose its voice? Some people believe that the size of a person's voice is directly related to his or her size. I strongly disagree with this (in most cases). It's most often a matter of how efficiently one uses one's voice. A baby is always, always, always *supporting* its voice—offering physical assistance to its throat by engaging muscle groups in the body that (1) keep the throat from contracting and tightening (thus disrupting airflow) and (2) prevent wear and tear on its larynx and vocal folds. Of course, a baby has one big advantage—it chooses a single note to sing. So to develop an efficient vocal technique, we need to relearn to sing as a baby cries—with high stakes on the one hand and physical support on the other.

## Legato

Singing has a language of its own: the language of legato. *Legato* is an Italian word that means "connected" or "bound together." So what are we binding together? From a musical standpoint, we are connecting individual notes to form a phrase, or a musical wave of sound (Figure 2). This is accompanied by a corresponding group of words that are strung together into a sentence (which I prefer to think of as a thought). Therefore, we have a complete legato concept—a line of music partnering with a line of text that communicates something both visceral and specific (Figure 3).

How is a legato phrase sustained vocally? It's carried over vowels rather than consonants. Try singing *k, t,* and *p.* These are known as *unvoiced* consonants. You'll find them to be vocally unsustainable. Now try singing *z* and *l*. These *voiced* consonants are vocally sustainable but won't work if you release your tongue from behind your front teeth or open your mouth. And because singing is akin to wailing, you want to be opening your mouth and *releasing* a sound. Hence the vast majority of the sound we generate to execute and sustain a legato line is delivered via vowels. Another way of describing and practicing singing would be to think of it as exaggerated, or *slow-motion*, speech.

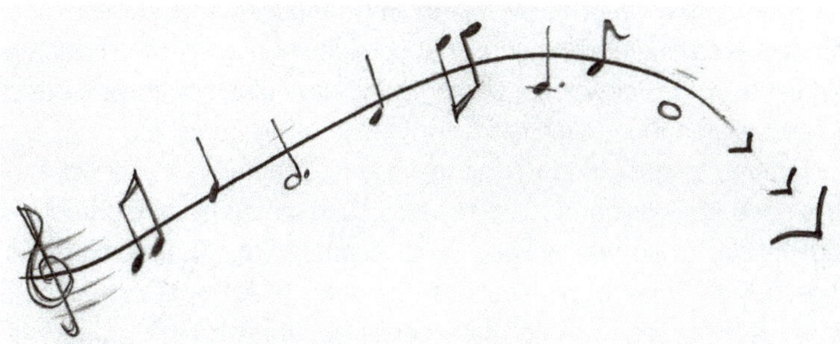

**Figure 2** Legato line of music.

**Figure 3** Legato line of text.

# Diphthongs

Because sound is carried along on the wings of vowels, we must be careful to analyze everything that goes into the production of a vowel sound, including—in the English language especially—diphthongs. A diphthong is the second of two consecutive vowels composed in the same syllable that generally are pronounced after an unstressed syllable or at the end of a syllable. For example, the sound known as a schwa is commonly heard in English speech. It sounds like *uh* and is formed at the back of the tongue, toward the throat. When you say the word "love," are you adding a schwa? If you say it slowly, does it sound like *laa-uhv*? The second, or shadow, vowel sound following the *ah* is the *uh*. Ideally, when singing, you need to focus on expanding the primary, or pure, vowel sound of the word (in this case, *ah*) and quickly dispensing with the diphthong at the end.

Or consider the word "why." Does it come out sounding like *whaa-yee*? The secondary vowel sound that we need to avoid in this case is the *ee*. It may feel odd at first to sing pure vowels and delay and sometimes eliminate diphthongs, but pure-vowel singing is the bedrock of great singing. Believe me, singing with heavy diphthongs as a basic technique will sound much more odd and possibly comedic.

I referred to our friend Kermit the frog in Chapter 1. If you want to do a good impression of Kermit's voice, just use as many diphthongs as possible, close your vowels, and lengthen your final consonants (especially *r*). Think of his sound in the song "Rainbow Connection": the lyrics "Why are there so many songs about rainbows?" come out as *Waa-uh-yee aa-uh-rrr theh-uh-rrr so ma-uh-nee saa-uhngz uh-bowt ray-uhn-bowz.* When sung by Kermit, it's charming. When we use it as a vocal technique, it's unintentionally ridiculous.

Diphthongs must be delayed in singing, because singing vowels should never fall back toward the throat. Think of delaying the diphthong portion of a word until you form the final consonant (in the case of the word "love," the *v*; in the case of the word "rainbows," the *s*). Pure vowels are a vital component to any legato line because they keep the sounds opening instead of closing. So we want to sing the lyrics to "Rainbow Connection" like this: *Waah yaah rtheh rsaaw mehnee saawng zaahbaauh trayhnbohz.*

## EXERCISE 17: SING IN SLOW MOTION

- Choose a line of text from a song you know or are working on, preferably a ballad such as "If I Loved You" (see page 7).
- Speak the line, without singing it, as slowly as possible, lingering on the vowel portion of every syllable, so that "If I loved you" becomes *liiiiii faaaaaaaaaah ylaaaaaaaaaaaaaaaah vdyeeooo*. Make sure you are not overly aggressive (explosive) with the initial consonant or vowel of each word. This will break up your airflow and interrupt your legato line.
- Point the index finger of one hand at your own shoulder. Then speak the line again, as slowly as possible, while smoothly moving your index finger away from your body. At the end of the line, your arm should be fully extended. Make sure your index finger moves forward at a steady, undisturbed rate with the text. This will help your body know what a legato line feels like.
- What do you notice about the amount of time you spent on the vowel portions of the words? Make sure to linger on the pure vowels of each word and not the diphthongs.
- Sing the words just as you spoke them. Do you feel that you are deliberately lengthening the pure vowels and delaying the diphthongs?
- Speak the line again. Do so slowly while pointing and moving your index finger forward, making sure to speak the line on the approximate pitches of the melody. What do you observe about the sound? Does your jaw feel like it is opening or closing? Does the sound feel smooth or choppy? Try to bind together your sounds as smoothly as possible, using the consonants to open the jaw and vowels.
- Now sing the line as if it were a natural extension of the way you just spoke it. Does it feel smoother? More released?

## Single point of resonance

When we sing, it is vital that we find a *point of focus* for our sound as it goes from the vocal cords (our phonators) to the audience. How does the sound travel? It is delivered via resonance. Resonance in the human body acts as an amplifier for the phonator—the larynx. This amplification is delivered via vibrations. Our bodies include many resonators that naturally magnify and project our sound. The primary resonators are located in the skull and the chest, where a multitude of small bones vibrate and thus project the voice. Some resonators, including the nasal cavities, make sounds that can be unattractive in singing and can be bypassed. When employing our resonators, we arrive at a big decision: do we try to project, or *move* the voice into these resonators, depending on the pitches we are singing, or do we trust that the appropriate or maximal resonance will be available to us if we *allow* our resonators to follow the voice?

Think of driving a car with a manual transmission, or stick shift, versus one with an automatic transmission. We can either constantly move the gear-shift knob around, as we do with a manual transmission, or we can let the car do the shifting for us. The same goes for the voice: we can either choose to physically direct the voice to a place in our bodies—a technique that some teachers call placement—or we can *allow* the resonators and various pitches to automatically engage if we are diligent about finding a reliable focus point. I highly recommend the automatic transmission method, because you'll find it simpler and much more consistent. After all, you will eventually be doing this on stage, and if you use an overcomplicated technique, you won't be able to think about anything else. I want you to feel like you can let your voice soar, not be stuck plodding on the ground.

The notion of placement has never made sense to me because sound moves—well, at the speed of sound. When singing, we don't have enough time to shift gears and transmit the sound to a different resonating cavity. Instead, I'm looking for a place to *focus* the sound, regardless of the pitch, using my mind as much as my body.

Imagine a small circle right above your upper lip and below your nose. Now place your index fingers right above your ears and firmly (but not violently) clench your teeth together. Can you feel a muscle that slightly pushes against your fingers? This place on your skull, combined with the spot above your upper lip, is an ideal location for your point of resonance.

Imagine your sound sliding *downhill* from above your ears and exiting right below your nose. This will keep the voice away from your throat and instruct your body to engage enough space for the voice to freely exit without too much conscious lifting of soft tissues, including your soft palate.

## EXERCISE 18: FIND A SINGLE POINT OF RESONANCE

- Begin to sigh as lightly as possible out of your nose with your jaw gently closed.
- Let all the air exit the nose before you allow any sound to escape.
- Add tone to the sigh while keeping it very light.
- Now allow the sigh to evolve into light humming. Organize the humming into a very simple song or nursery rhyme ("Happy Birthday," "Mary Had a Little Lamb," or something similar).
- Where do you feel the sound vibrating without forcing it? Is it near your throat, your mouth, or is it closer to your cheekbones and nasal cavities?
- Now gently open your jaw, but keep the air and sound flowing *only* through the nose (continuing your humming of the simple song). Your tongue will feel very high in the back of your mouth, in contact with your uvula. Keep the tip of the tongue lightly in contact with the inner gums below your lower teeth.
- Now, with your jaw open, *imagine* you are humming an *ee* vowel, but continue keeping the air and sound exiting through your nose.
- As slowly as possible, allow the *ee* vowel to evolve and shift from exiting through the nose to exiting through the mouth. Let the tongue stay undisturbed and inactivated. This will allow the uvula to lift away from the tongue rather than vice versa.
- Where do you feel the *ee* vowel being formed? Where is the exit point of the *ee*?
- *This* is how I want you to develop the sense of a single point of resonance. You should repeat this exercise as often as you can until finding this point becomes second nature to you.

## The vocal tract

Your vocal tract is the place where sound is produced and channeled out of your body (Figure 4). It includes the *larynx*, the *pharynx*, and the *oral and nasal cavities*. The larynx (the voice box) is a structure made of flexible cartilage located above the trachea (the windpipe). The pharynx is a soft-tissue cavity behind the nose and mouth, connecting them to the esophagus and larynx. It is a flexible and malleable area capable of producing a great variety of vocal colors. The oral cavity is the fleshy

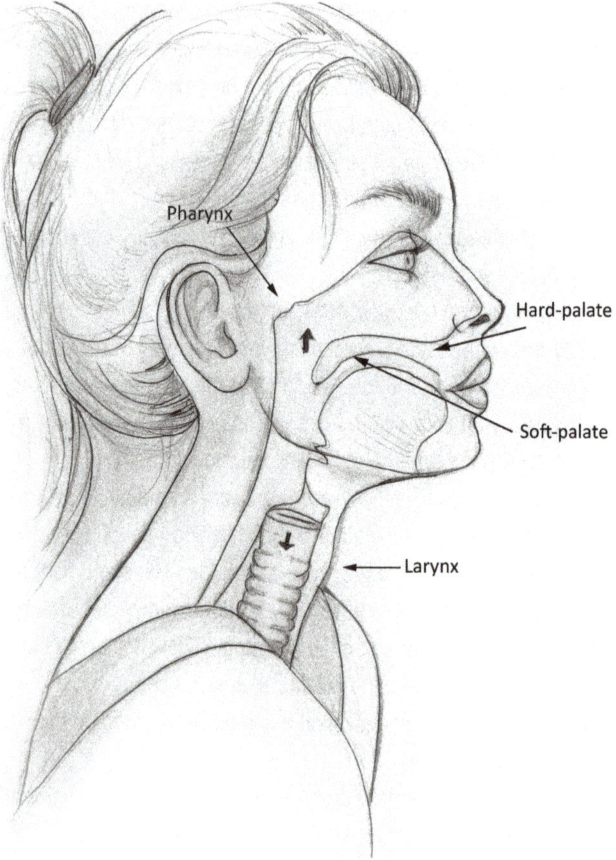


**Figure 4** The vocal tract.

and bony interior of the mouth, and the nasal cavities are chambers located behind and above the nose. It is important to note that the nasal cavity is part of the vocal tract *only* when the pharynx and soft palate (Figure 4) are not engaged. The vocal tract is not a fundamental resonator, but when it is engaged in a long, expansive way, it gives the voice access to a greater amount of resonators and resonance.

You may have heard the expression "sing with an open throat." For several reasons, I don't tell my students to do this. First, your throat is essentially a channel made of cartilage topped by a narrow and inflexible aperture. Because the channel through which the voice travels is itself constructed of cartilage, its width cannot be increased, hence it cannot be opened. When you try to "open your throat," you attempt to create space for the voice to escape. Most likely you will instead lower your tongue, which will create *negative space*, pulling the voice down and back, the opposite of setting it free.

Think of a *crescent* or letter *c* beginning at the lower larynx, traveling almost *behind* the neck and cresting *behind* and *above* your ears before it slides downward toward the space between your upper lip and nose. The voice can travel freely along this crescent to the vital head resonators and away from unattractive nasality. Ideally we want to sing with a long vocal tract, or column. This means that we need the maximum *vertical* stretch between the larynx and the pharynx. This stretch is achieved not by pulling or pushing but rather by sustaining our primary vowels.

## The soft palate

The *soft palate* inhabits the rear of the roof of your mouth and is distinguished from your *hard palate*, located in the front of the roof of your mouth, because it does not contain bone. It is flexible and useful in singing because it blocks the nasal cavities when it is activated. Many well-intentioned voice teachers and choir directors have made the "lifting of the soft palate" a cornerstone of their prescribed vocal technique. I think it's born from a desire to cultivate a round, beautiful sound, a goal I wholeheartedly agree with. Unfortunately, in many singers, this effort to "make space" results in the lowering of the tongue. This adds throat tension and prevents the voice from reaching the important upper resonators, resulting in flat singing because of the absence of overtones.

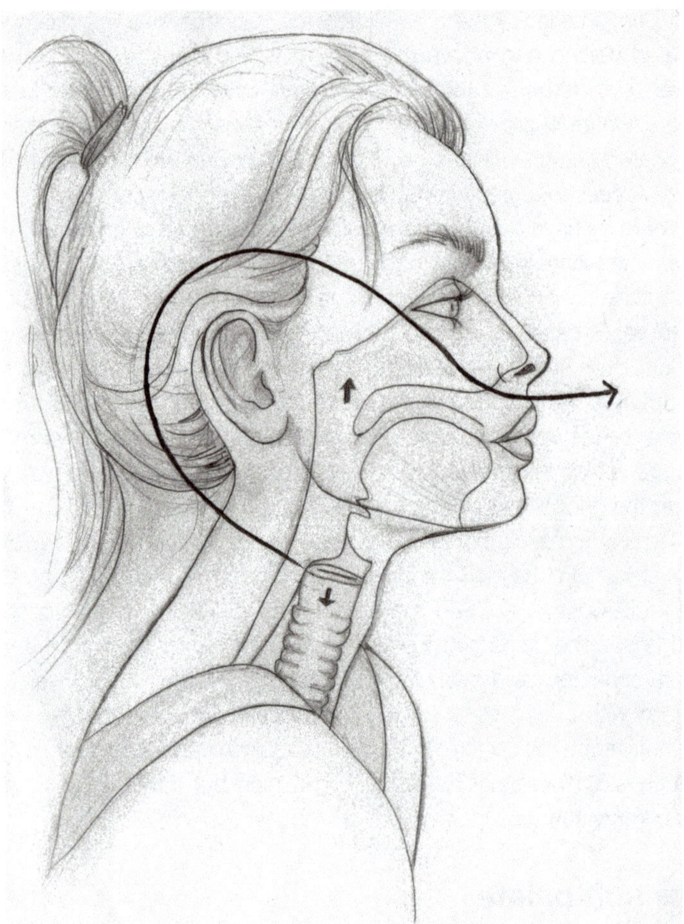

**Figure 5** Vocal trajectory.

My thinking on the soft palate may be considered controversial by some singers and teachers, but if you're raising your soft palate while simultaneously closing off your pharynx, you will be forced to sing and form your vowels by manipulating your tongue and lower throat. The technique I am teaching you, by contrast, will activate your soft palate and pharyngeal space in a way that *allows* the vocal tract to open (Figure 5). This will clear a *round* path for your voice.

## EXERCISE 19: DISENGAGE YOUR TONGUE

If you fell asleep in a chair with your head hanging back and your mouth open, what would be the position of your tongue? Because the tongue is primarily part of your digestive system, it would probably be disengaged, and your breathing would occur in the spaces *above* and *around* it, possibly including your nose. To discover what a disengaged tongue feels like when you're awake, practice this exercise.

- While looking in a mirror, *gently* snore and observe the relationship between your tongue and the soft tissues surrounding it.
- While snoring, practice keeping the tongue from activating.
- Snoring while inhaling will train you to allow your soft palate, uvula, and pharyngeal tissues to activate and expand away from your tongue.
- After you've done this a few times, practice yawning while looking in the mirror.
- Then inhale and try to lift your soft palate
- Exhale while saying *aaaaaaaahhhhh.* Make sure to drop your jaw enough to make the back of your mouth visible.
- Observe what happens to your tongue when you attempt to raise your soft palate. Does it naturally draw itself back and down?

## Vowels

To achieve a round path for the voice, we need to practice singing vowels that are primarily formed in the pharynx. I like to think of vowels as the colors we use to paint the sounds we choose to sing. This includes a diversity of sounds that I'll refer to on a scale from bright to dark. In this paradigm, I think of the *ee* as the brightest vowel sound, followed by the *ay, ah, oh*, and *oo* sounds, with *oo* being the darkest. I'll take this a step further and divide these vowel sounds into two categories: *closed* and *open*.

*Closed* vowel sounds require less space than open vowel sounds. Interestingly, our brightest (*ee*) and darkest (*oo*) vowel sounds can both be categorized as *closed*.

*Open* vowel sounds require enough space to keep them from getting stuck in the throat. This space is mostly created by dropping the jaw. Open vowel sounds are also the likeliest to seduce the tongue into an overly low position, which will bleed an unintended schwa or *uh* quality into the vowel—leading to an overly spread or nasal sound. Our two primary *open* vowel sounds are *ah* and *oh*.

To ensure that you are giving the vowels enough space, put the tip of one finger in your mouth and close your teeth around it gently. That is the ideal amount of space you should allow when you're singing closed vowels (*ee, ay, oo*). Now put two fingers (stacked vertically) into your mouth and close your teeth around them gently. That's the ideal amount of space you should give open vowel sounds (*ah, oh*) when singing.

## Spreading

When you sing, do you make a lot of uncomfortable faces? Does it look like you are grimacing or forcing a demonically wide smile? If so, you are most likely using your cheeks and mouth to pull a compromised (stuck) voice out of your throat, or *spreading* (Figure 6). Unless you are purposely cultivating a flat and nasal sound, make sure that the corners of your mouth (where the top and bottom lips connect) are never moving outward. Try to keep the corners of your mouth gathered, and replace the habit of spreading with dropping your jaw. This more vertical trajectory will help keep the entire vocal tract long and narrow, giving you more vocal freedom and power.

So how do we find a consistency of resonance and sound in spite of having to sing vowels that vary greatly in brightness and openness? The following exercise will take us to the next step.

## EXERCISE 20: SPEAK OPEN AND CLOSED VOWELS

- Point your index finger at your face, with your hand in the shape of an imaginary pistol.
- Insert your index finger between your upper and lower front teeth.
- Slightly drop your jaw away from your finger and make an *ee* sound. Make sure you don't clench your jaw or activate your tongue.
- Repeat the exercise but this time try the *ay* vowel. Make sure you don't spread your lips and cheeks.
- Repeat with the *oo* vowel. Is it hard not to lower your tongue or bite your finger on this vowel?
- In our lower and middle ranges (which differ from person to person), this is an excellent way of determining how much space is required to sing a closed vowel.
- Again point your index finger toward your face but also extend your middle finger, with your hand in the shape of a two-fingered pistol.
- Insert your index and middle fingers between your upper and lower front teeth.
- Slightly drop your jaw away from your fingers and make an *ah* sound. Make sure you don't clench your jaw or activate your tongue. Also, be sure not to spread your lips or cheeks. Instead think of your lips (especially the lower lip) gently puckering away from your face.
- Repeat, but this time make an *oh* sound. What feels different about this sound from the *ah*? Think of the *oh* as having the same height and depth as *ah* but occurring slightly more forward and puckered away from the face.

This is an excellent way to determine the ideal amount of space you'll need to sing open vowels throughout your *entire* vocal range (with the exception of extreme high notes).

**Figure 6** Vocal spreading.

## EXERCISE 21: SING OPEN AND CLOSED VOWELS

- On a piano, an electronic keyboard, or a piano app, find and play middle C (C4) if you are female or the C an octave below it (C3) if you are male (see Figure 11 in the Appendix).
- Using the one-finger, two-finger method in Exercise 20, sing *ee ay ah oh oo*, in that exact order, on the appropriate C note. Use one finger for *ee, ay*, and *oo* and two fingers for *ah* and *oh*.
- What do you notice about the jaw-space-finger relationship from vowel to vowel? Can you keep your tongue from dropping in the

back on certain vowels (especially the open ones)? Think of your jaw dropping like a wooden nutcracker soldier (Figure 7). This will make it easier to keep from clenching your jaw and spreading your cheeks.

- Staying in the key of C, sing a five-note scale on each vowel sound. Start on C, then go to D, E, F, and G, then back down. Make sure to follow the same one-finger, two-finger method.
- What do you notice or observe? Does something physically engage that you didn't intend to engage? Does your tongue begin lowering? Are your cheeks spreading? Is your jaw trying to close? Are you contorting your facial muscles? If so, repeat and choose the high tongue, gently puckered lips and jaw over whatever else is engaging.

**Figure 7** Gathering.

## What is support?

Have you ever heard a teacher or singer talk about "breath support"? To me, this is an oversimplified and misleading term. It doesn't describe how a flexible support system should actually work. Housed in your larynx are two tiny folds of tissue—your vocal folds, or vocal cords—which vibrate with the passage of air. Clearly breath is an important *component* in singing. But the actual voice originates in the throat, not the lungs. So my question to you is this: what are you supporting? Are you supporting your breath? Or are you supporting your throat (i.e., your voice)?

If you chose the former, why would you choose to support air rather than the part of your body that actually does the singing? To me, breath and support are two vital but *separate* components of great singing. In my case, the thing I'm supporting is definitely my throat, not my breath.

Let's examine the definition of "support." According to the eleventh edition of *Merriam-Webster's Collegiate Dictionary*, the verb "support" means, among other things: "assist, help" and "hold up or serve as a foundation or prop for."[1] Both sound about right. For our purposes, I'm going to define "support" as: "offering physical assistance to the throat by engaging muscle groups that redirect energy away from the throat, allowing for laryngeal flexibility and unrestricted airflow."

To visualize this, picture yourself standing in a pool of shoulder-deep water holding a medium-size beach ball. Now imagine that you pull the beach ball under the water and hold it below your sternum. What happens when you release the ball? Does it stay under the water? Or does it shoot up and out like a geyser? *This* is very much like the relationship between singing and support. In this analogy, your voice is the beach ball and the physical pulling and holding the ball under water is the support. You can assume that without support, your voice and physical energy will shoot upward and lock your throat as though they were tightening a noose. Does this sound familiar? When you sing, do you feel a lot of pressure in your throat? Does your voice get easily fatigued or hoarse? Are you making a lot of strange, contorted faces when you sing? This is *all* the result of a crucial need for consistent support.

---

[1] *Merriam-Webster's Collegiate Dictionary*, 11th ed., s.v. "support."

When you practice a conscious habit of supporting everything you do vocally on a daily basis—including talking on the phone, chatting with your friends over coffee, interacting with clerks at the store—vocal fatigue will become a thing of the past.

## The role of the lungs

Your lungs are basically two bags filled with tubes and blood vessels. When expanded, they are filled with fresh oxygen, which immediately gets sent into the blood and delivered as food and fuel to the cells of the body. The body then changes this air to carbon dioxide, which is essentially cell poop, and sends it back to the lungs. Based on this sequence of events, please fill in the blank below:

When the lungs are expanded, their internal air pressure is ________ than when they are contracted.

A. Greater
B. Less

You are likely picturing the lungs as two balloons, so my guess is you picked A. But you would be wrong.

The lungs are like an instantly inflatable raft that has an open hole or tear. If you put a person in such a raft, the pressure would increase and force air quickly through the hole. Have you ever impatiently sat on an air mattress to empty the air? That's basically what happens when you breathe. The lungs are the mattress, and the diaphragm is your body weight applying the pressure. The lungs expand and contract, but they are completely helpless without the assistance of the diaphragm.

## The role of the diaphragm

The diaphragm is a flexible, parachute-like muscle that connects to the body at the lower ribs, from sternum to spine. Its primary function is to assist in the act of breathing, and without it, your lungs would not function. The problem is that the diaphragm does not contain the same kinds of nerve endings as skeletal muscles do. If I told you to raise your arm, you'd be able to voluntarily do it and feel it. But if I told you to inhale, what would happen? I'm sure you'd be able to take in a breath. But could you actually *feel* your diaphragm? I don't think so. The only times I've ever felt my diaphragm in action were when I had the wind knocked out of me while playing sports. In those scary and painful moments, I recall feeling the panic of waiting for my diaphragm to "reboot" so that I could resume breathing.

Have you ever used a bellows when making a fire? A bellows is an air bag topped by two handles that, when pushed together, force the bag to blow out a stream of air. The bellows refills with air when the handles are pulled back apart. Similarly, when we inhale deeply, our diaphragm lowers, our ribs expand, and our lungs vacuum in fresh oxygen. And upon exhalation, the diaphragm releases upward like a parachute into the lungs. The ribs contract, and we expel carbon dioxide. So the diaphragm, like a bellows, is the engine of breath. Please fill in the blank in the following sentence:

When you are singing (and thus releasing air), your diaphragm should be pushing _____.

A. Out
B. In
C. Up
D. Down

If you answered B or C, I understand your logic, but you would be wrong. Yes, when we exhale, the diaphragm moves up, because the lungs cannot expel air without diaphragmatic pressure. But we want to *delay* and *extend* this upward movement. After all, a phrase (or breath) of song usually lasts a lot longer than a spoken sentence, so we need technique that supports us beyond everyday speech. We know that air pressure in the lungs (and the throat) increases when the diaphragm pushes into the lungs, so we need to *override* this event. Therefore, when we sing, we need to try to hold the diaphragm in the down position—so D is the correct answer.

The muscle groups known as the internal and external obliques and the quadratus lumborum play a key role in this process. The obliques wrap around the sides of your lower abdomen, connecting to your abdominal muscles in the front. They feel like and function as a girdle—or, in the more modern version, an undergarment made by Spanx. They also act as an *antagonist* to the diaphragm when they're contracted, so we need to allow them to fully expand and lengthen upon inhalation.

## EXERCISE 22: LOCATE YOUR DIAPHRAGM

- Place both index fingers directly under your sternum and trace them in opposite directions under your lowest ribs until you reach your spine. This roughly covers the attachment points of your diaphragm to your body. It also demarcates the position of the diaphragm when you have inhaled the maximum amount of air possible. If you've ever heard someone say something like "breathe low," you should be aware that your lungs are located inside your rib cage, and your lowest ribs are as low as your diaphragm can stretch, so it's physically impossible to breathe any "lower" than your ribs.
- Place your hands on your back, immediately above your pelvis. Inhale deeply and slowly until you feel something push your hands slightly outward. This is your *oblique* muscle system releasing and allowing the perimeter of your thoracic cavity (torso) to expand, clearing space for the ribs, diaphragm, and internal organs. It is also the location of your lowest (floating) ribs. The diaphragm attaches lower in the back than it does in the front. Picture a tuxedo coat with a high front and tails in the back.

How does this all relate to the question of air pressure and, more importantly, support? As you know, your larynx is essentially a tube with a very narrow aperture at the top. (Have you ever heard of someone choking to death on a peanut? That's because this opening is no wider than a dime!) Your larynx and trachea connect and sit right above your lungs: it is as if the larynx were a flexible, accordion-like flute perched vertically above a geyser full of high-pressure air. What would happen to the flute if the geyser went into a full eruption? Would the air pass *through* the flute, or would the air push the entire flute upward? It would definitely push the entire flute upward, and this is exactly what happens to your throat when you sing without support. Instead of funneling air *through* your throat and vocal cords, you force the entire throat upward into a semilocked position.

## Attacco della voce

*Attacco della voce* (Italian for “vocal attack”) is the moment when your vocal cords begin to vibrate. We can also call this the vocal *onset*. When this happens without support, it will usually result in a contracted, *glottal* sound. This comes from an explosion of air from behind a closed *glottis* (the opening between the vocal cords), creating a percussive pulse that often includes a slight grunt. To avoid this, you need to learn how to support your throat *before* you make sound. Your larynx and vocal cords should always contain an appropriate amount of air at the onset, as if you were threading a needle of air through the throat instead of causing an explosion. This keeps the throat unlocked and flexible enough to sing a phrase of music freely and beautifully. So think of your support system as a tape delay—remember to always engage it the moment *before* you sing. Every phrase you sing should be sung in this order: *breathe, support, sing.*

## The role of the belly

Picture a pair of sumo wrestlers. What part of their bodies do they use to push their opponents out of the ring? It’s their gargantuan bellies. This pushing is similar to what you do when you are supporting your voice from the diaphragm. The difference is that you shouldn’t need sumo-wrestler-level force to support your larynx. What you need is an ample *counterbalance* to the amount of energy and air required to sing any phrase of music.

### EXERCISE 23: USE YOUR BELLY

- **Find a piano or piece of furniture that comes up to your belly, between your belly button and sternum.**
- ***Without thrusting with your legs*, try to push the object away from you with your belly.**

- **Were you able to move the object? Were you inhaling or exhaling?**
- **Repeat, but this time, if you were inhaling, try to move the object while exhaling.**
- **Did this make it more challenging to move the object? Were you successful?**
- **What was the physical sensation? What muscle groups did you use?**

It's useful to attempt to move something large and heavy as a way to awaken your physical awareness and practice allowing your belly (and, in turn, your diaphragm) to forcefully activate and push out. Unfortunately, we can't be pushing into heavy objects while singing on stage, although it might be hilarious to see. Let's find a better and subtler way of supporting from the diaphragm that doesn't require so much effort.

First we'll replace the verb "push" with the verb "lean." The Italian word for "lean" is *appoggio*, which is commonly used by singers as a synonym for "support." Certain senses of the verb "lean" are synonymous with the words "tilt" and "bend." Do these words imply anything pushed or forceful to you? They shouldn't, because great technique should never require us to work too hard. Remember, technique should be an *undetectable* story-delivery system. Supporting should be something easeful.

If we need to think of ourselves as leaning, then what, exactly, are we leaning toward or away from? In singing, we are leaning air pressure and contractive muscularity (tension) away from the throat *and* we are leaning the diaphragm away from the lungs.

*Appoggio* can also be used as a noun. For our purposes, it refers to a belly that is fully expanded (Figure 8). I've heard many descriptions of the ideal *appoggio*, including the plop, Thanksgiving dinner tummy, and my personal favorite, the alien—as in a creature attempting to push its way out of your abdomen.

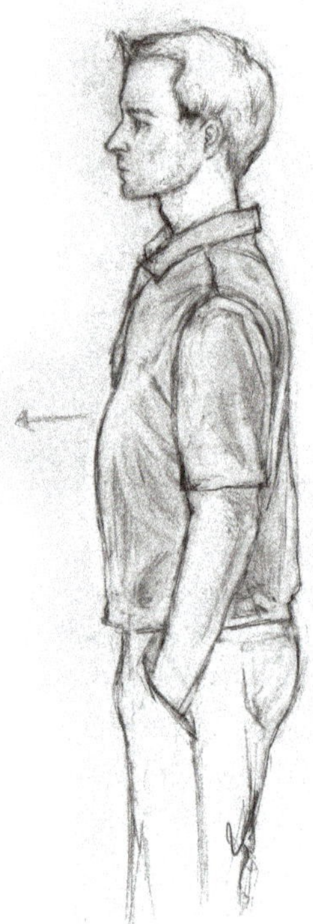

**Figure 8** *Appoggio.*

## EXERCISE 24: FIND YOUR *APPOGGIO* USING A MUSIC STAND

- Turn a music stand backward toward you at an approximately eighty-degree angle, with the top of the music stand tilting toward you (see Figure 9).
- Stand about an inch away from the music stand, with the top of the stand just below the height of your sternum.
- Blow all the air out of your body vigorously. On the next inhalation allow your upper abdomen to expand into the top of the music stand. This should gently tilt the music stand forward and off

**Figure 9** *Appoggio* music stand.

the supporting legs that are facing you. You should be able to lean the stand forward without tipping it over.

- Repeat the previous step, but this time add phonation, such as "ahhhh." Make sure you begin tilting the music stand slightly *before* you make the sound.
- Repeat the previous step again, but this time, sing a complete line of a song. Do this on one breath, all the while tilting the music stand forward with your *appoggio*.
- Repeat the previous step again, but this time, sing your entire song. Always lean the music stand away from you at the end of every breath, *before* every vocal onset. If you find this challenging or aren't able to recover your support before you sing,

slow down. This will train your body to be engaging in a form of *intradiaphragmatic* support at all times while you sing.

- Make sure that the recovery moment between breaths is not a huge event. In short, you shouldn't lose much of your *appoggio* when you inhale.

If you'd like to accelerate the speed at which you assimilate this into your singing process, I strongly recommend you begin practicing this when you speak. It will give your voice depth, power, and freshness on stage.

## EXERCISE 25: FIND YOUR *APPOGGIO* USING A GENTLY CLOSED FIST

- Gently close one hand into a fist.
- Softly place your fist on your upper abdominals, immediately below your sternum.
- Gently press your fist into the area.
- Begin moving your fist in a small circle.
- Allowing your ribs to expand, breathe into your fist while keeping your ribs expanded.
- Press your fist slightly more firmly into your upper abdomen. Try to press your upper back into your fist.
- Repeat the previous step, but this time press your abdomen into your fist while exhaling.
- Repeat the previous step, but this time speak immediately following the expansion of your abdomen into your fist. Make sure you continue this expansion to the end of whatever phrase you are speaking.
- Repeat the previous step, but this time sing an entire phrase of a song, diligently expanding your upper abdomen until the end of the phrase.

## Kinetic chains

An excellent vocal technique requires the activation and employment of an efficient *kinetic chain*. By this I mean that we are recruiting specific interlinking muscles, bones, and tissues to spark a chain of events that will result in reliably consistent singing. These muscles, bones, and tissues include but are not limited to the ribs, spine, obliques, glutes, lats, levators (upper back), sternocleidomastoids (neck), pharynx, jaw, and diaphragm.

Similarly, to demonstrate how things should *not* be done, we can recruit a less efficient kinetic chain that will also produce consistent results—i.e., reliably bad singing. Perhaps the most commonly activated physiological group in this category is what a former teacher of mine unaffectionately referred to as "the tongue, the throat, and the abs are buddies" group. The obvious sign of its activation is a wild, unstable tongue that is flailing and thrashing, especially on vowels. Look a bit closer and you may notice the bulging veins of a tight, constricted neck and throat. What you probably can't see are the clenching and contracted abdominal muscles that squeeze the life out of the lungs and prevent the diaphragm from expanding. Let me assure you that having tight, contracted "six-pack" abs (especially the top ones) is a surefire way to sing with a locked throat and tense tongue. This type of contraction-based kinetic chain of events is what I call an antisupport technique. If you like pushing until your voice becomes fatigued, hoarse, fugly, and possibly damaged, this is the technique for you.

### EXERCISE 26: EXPAND YOUR SPINE AND RIBS

- **Find the place between your femur and pelvis on the front of your body where your leg inserts into the pelvis at the hip socket. This is your "true waist," where your torso ends and your legs begin.**
- **Allow your head and torso to fold toward the floor from this place—not from your belly button, also known as your "fashion waist."**

- Allow your head and arms to gently dangle. With each breath, keep releasing the spine and head.
- Slowly let your hands and knuckles (if possible) sweep the floor in a gentle figure eight.
- Observe your breath as you exhale and inhale. See if you can feel your lower back ribs expanding on every inhalation. This expansion is occurring in and around your oblique muscles.
- Keep breathing deeply and imagine that each breath allows more space between every vertebra in your back and neck.
- Phonate the *ah* vowel, as if sighing. See if you can keep your ribs expanding while you phonate and sigh. Also observe that your front ribs, sternum, and the front of your diaphragm are pushing slightly into your femurs.
- Repeat the previous steps and observe what happens to your obliques and lower abdominal muscles. Do they begin to contract the longer you sustain the *ah* vowel? This is okay: they eventually must contract because that is their function in the exhalation of air.
- Repeat the previous steps and allow the obliques and lower abs to contract while keeping your ribs and upper abdominals expanding. Can you feel the push–pull relationship between the muscle groups?
- Repeat the previous steps ten times, continuing to allow your fingers and knuckles to gently sway and sweep the floor in front of you.
- One vertebra at a time, rise back to a standing position, your neck and head coming up last.
- Standing, repeat the sighing of the *ah* vowel. Can you feel the same depth and expansion of your breath and phonation that you felt in the bent-over position? Can you keep your spine and neck long? More important, can you keep your ribs and upper abdominals moving *outward* while your obliques and lower abs begin to pull *inward*?

## High, low, and tilted larynx

The larynx sits immediately below a wishbone-like piece of cartilage called the *hyoid*. Most pinched and constricted singing occurs when the larynx is pushed upward, into the hyoid. This leaves little to no room for the larynx to tilt backward, which is how it assists the vocal cords in lengthening and thus producing high notes. High laryngeal singing leads to fatigue, vocal nodules, and potentially permanent anatomical damage.

When you practice the following exercise, it is vital that you engage the support system covered earlier in this chapter. If not, your larynx will move straight upward as the result of an explosion of air pressure. Be sure not to force or hold down the throat with your muscles, though. Forcing the larynx to stay down is just as dangerous to your physiology in the long run as singing with a high larynx.

### EXERCISE 27: SUPPORT YOUR LARYNX

- Look at your throat in a mirror.
- Gently massage your throat and try to locate your larynx below your jaw, in the middle of your neck. In men, it is directly behind the Adam's apple.
- While observing the larynx, gently and deeply snore with a complete inhalation of air. What effect did this have on the larynx? Did it move?
- Repeat the previous step, making sure that the snore is deep and vigorous enough to cause the larynx to move downward, toward the clavicle.
- Repeat the previous step, this time exhaling with a gentle sigh on an *ah* vowel. What did you observe this time? Did the larynx stay in a lower position? Or did it immediately move upward?

- Repeat the previous step until you feel air moving freely through your throat and the larynx staying in a low position upon phonation. Can you feel that your sound now includes more depth and a sensation of core power?
- Repeat the previous step while singing a phrase of a song. Is this more challenging? Can you keep the larynx largely undisturbed throughout the phrase? What notes of the phrase make it difficult? Are you still supporting from the diaphragm *before* and *during* the entire phrase?

## EXERCISE 28: IMAGINE A TROMBONE

A great way to practice singing with a stable yet flexible throat is to practice sliding from low notes to high notes and from high notes to low notes as if you were playing a trombone.

- With your mouth in an embouchure (soft pucker), imagine that you are holding a trombone next to your head.
- In the key of C major, sing the notes between middle C and the E just above it—an interval of a major third (*do, mi, do*). Make sure your voice travels smoothly between notes (see Figure 11 in the Appendix).
- As the pitch gets higher, begin pulling the slide of an imaginary trombone with one hand horizontally toward your face and ear. Manipulate the slide away from you as your pitch descends.
- Repeat the first two steps twelve times.
- How does this feel?
- Repeat the previous four steps, but this time sing the notes between middle C and the G just above it—an interval of a major fifth (*do-so-do)*.

- **Repeat the previous steps, but this time sing the entire octave between middle C and the C above it *(do-do-do)*. Make sure to only do as many repetitions as your throat and support can tolerate before things feel overly strained. Can you sense that your are *allowing* the pitches to be full and released instead of *placing* each note?**

## Breath

Breathing is something we all do every few seconds of every day of our lives, whether we are asleep or awake. It's not something we have to spend a lot of time practicing. That said, it is a core component of singing, because the passage of air is what activates the vibration of the vocal cords. A colleague of mine once shared a story he'd heard about the famous dramatic tenor Franco Corelli. Allegedly Maestro Corelli was once asked about his breathing technique. To this he replied, "My breathing technique? I don't understand your question. I just take a breath." Although this may be an apocryphal story, I find the gist of it completely understandable. When it comes to technique, it should be simple! Anything we do on stage should be something that doesn't require a complex set of steps to accomplish.

Open your ribs and allow your lungs to fill with air. When you purposely inhale like this, you are lengthening a process that happens quite quickly when it's involuntary. The lowering of your diaphragm creates a vacuum effect in the lungs, which fills them almost instantaneously.

What's more important is how we *exhale* when singing. Think of the air you expel as having momentum and inevitability. Don't try to conserve your air or mete it out. Assuming you are now employing a technique of support (see page 48), once you've established an efficient and inexplosive vocal onset, you need to get *all* the air out of your lungs on every phrase you sing. This will trigger the body to *naturally* expand and refill with a "full tank" of air.

What I'm suggesting you do is get out of the habit of holding your breath. You need an energetic and accelerating airflow to sing dynamically *and* create the conditions under which each new breath can be efficient and deep.

## EXERCISE 29: EXHALE ON *FFFFFF*

- Purposely expel all the air in your lungs while making a *ffffff* sound. Using the *ffffff* accelerates the emptying of your lungs.
- After every ounce of breath is out, open your mouth and allow your body to refill with air. Make sure your lower ribs are expanding.
- What do you observe about your inhalation moment? Are you tempted to physically interfere and slow down the act of inhalation?
- Repeat the first two steps, making sure you don't allow the ribs to collapse on exhalation.
- Repeat the exercise five times. Observe your abdomen below your ribs during inhalation. Does it expand from the bottom up or the top down?

## EXERCISE 30: DRINK THE AIR AND POUR IT DOWN

I mentioned earlier the pitfalls of attempting to sing with an "open throat." Instead of trying to open your throat from the *inside*, let's allow the throat to relax and deepen from the *outside*.

- Imagine you are holding a pitcher containing air that is heavy and water-like. Tilt your head back and dump the air down your throat, allowing it to fill your lungs from the bottom to the top.

- **How does this *drinking* of air feel different from the way you usually breathe?**
- **Repeat the first step, and this time observe the sensation in the muscles of the neck. Did your neck feel as if it was widening and expanding? Make sure your imaginary pitcher contains almost *too much* imaginary heavy air.**
- **How does this feel?**
- **Repeat the first step again, but this time imagine that your lungs are bags. If you dumped *actual* water into a bag, it would definitely fill from the bottom to the top.**
- **How does this feel?**
- **Repeat the first step again, but this time don't tilt your head back. Rather, drop your jaw. Do you feel like you are getting a deeper breath? Does your throat feel wider, deeper, and more relaxed?**

When I'm teaching singing technique, I don't like to use the oversimplified expression "breath support" to describe what students should be doing. This is because singers need a technical solution to rely on if one element or the other—breath or support—isn't functioning particularly well. So if you think of breath and support as related to each other instead of inexorably connected, you'll be able to employ one of them to rescue and reawaken the other.

Think about it: if you physically perform an action, you need a moment of recovery before you can repeat the action. But when we're finished singing a phrase of music, what are we recovering? The simplest answer is *support*. We need support to free the breath and deliver the voice and the intention of the character to the audience and our scene partner(s).

## EXERCISE 31: RECOVER YOUR SUPPORT

- Sing two phrases (breaths) of your song.
- What happens between the two phrases? Are you audibly gasping for breath?
- Repeat the first step, using all the air in your lungs in the first phrase.
- Before you sing the second phrase, focus on recovering your support—i.e., the expansion of the diaphragm into a supple *appoggio*—and *allow* the lungs to refill with air.
- What did you observe? Did you get enough breath for the second phrase?
- Sing the entire song, focusing on the recovery of your support between each breath. Make sure that your inhalations aren't overly audible. A loud inhalation is indicative of a constricted throat, resulting in a shallow breath. I call this *straw breath* because it sounds like air is being sucked up through a straw.

# Vibrato

Vibrato is a slight variation in pitch, upward from the fundamental pitch being sustained, that can occur when singing. It is created by a slight trembling of the larynx. *True* vibrato is a result of technically efficient singing and enables the larynx to freely vibrate for long periods of time. The larynx vibrates as a result of a sympathetic oscillation of the muscles of the larynx. Have you ever felt your muscles begin to shake when doing some form of rigorous exercise? This is how your body keeps the muscle from tightening or cramping up. Singing with vibrato functions in a similar way for the throat muscles.

Vibrato is an essential feature of several singing styles. Operatic singing requires an almost perpetual *spinning*, as I call it, of the voice. Contemporary singing sometimes requires a straight tone (see below) that blossoms into a spin. I like to use the word "spin" to describe vibrato because it implies an unobstructed freedom of sound. For some people, the word "vibrato" connotes something created or manufactured. On the contrary, vibrato is not an added-on "special effect" but a *result* of good singing.

If you are singing rounded, supported vowels on released and dynamic air, you will likely produce a naturally spinning vibrato. There's no single way to trigger or jump-start your vibrato, and it may require patience and experimentation on your part.

Often, natural vibrato can be stifled by either too much or too little airflow through the throat. Sometimes there is simply too much air pressure below the larynx. This exercise might help you find the right balance between airflow and the activation of your vibrato.

## EXERCISE 32: FIND YOUR VIBRATO

- On a piano, an electronic keyboard, or a piano app, find and play the E below middle C (E3) if you are male or the E a third above middle C (E4) if you are female. Immediately to its right is the note F, which is a half step above E (see Figure 11 in the Appendix).
- On the *ee* vowel, sing the E pitch.
- Repeat the previous step, but this time sing the E pitch while alternating *slowly* back and forth with the F pitch approximately twelve times.
- Repeat the previous step, but this time slowly *accelerate* the shifting from E to F until you are moving from note to note as fast as possible.
- How does this feel? Are you making sure to engage your support while singing? Does it feel like the voice wants to begin to *spin* between the pitches?
- Repeat the first two steps, but begin shifting from E to F as rapidly as possible, making the E more important than the F.
- How does this feel? Does the voice feel as if it's beginning to spin? If so, simply sing the E, allowing the *spin* to replace the pitch change to F. If you're able to do this, you are singing with a true vibrato.

## EXERCISE 33: TURN THE SPINNING WHEEL

- Hold your hands below your sternum, a foot in front of your body.
- Make a fist with each hand. Extend the index fingers of both hands so that they are pointing toward each other.
- Using your forearms, begin slowly circling your index fingers around each other. Make sure they are circling away from your body.
- Begin slowly accelerating the circling of your fingers and forearms until they are moving as fast as you can move them. This should feel almost manically fast.
- Repeat the previous step, finding a speed that feels somewhat fast but smooth. The spinning wheel of your fingers and forearms should be very similar to what you consider a pleasing vibrato speed.
- Slowly, phonate an *ee* vowel in pulses for ten seconds. Try pulsing an *ee* once per second.
- Repeat the previous step, but this time synchronize the rotations of your index fingers with the pulses of the *ee*.
- Repeat again, synchronizing the *ee* pulses with your spinning hands, slowly accelerating the rate of the *ee* pulses.
- How does this feel? Make sure you are releasing your breath at the same rate of acceleration of your *ee* pulses and spinning hands.
- Repeat until you can match the *ee* pulses with the spinning rate you decided earlier was the speed of an ideal vibrato.
- How does this feel? Does a natural vibrato seem to blossom from the *ee* pulses? Do the pulses begin freely spinning?
- Repeat, but try pulsing and spinning with other vowels or words. Can you sustain the exercise on a single breath for longer than ten seconds? Can the voice continue to spin freely if you don't also spin your hands?
- Keep repeating and experimenting with this exercise until you sense a balance between your airflow and vibrato.

## Straight tone

A straight tone is produced by altering the balance of pressure between the diaphragm and the larynx. Bad straight-tone singing technique will always reveal itself when vibrato is reintroduced to the sound. The reintroduction sounds unstable and is sometimes wobbly, sometimes machine gun-like. This happens because the straight tone wasn't being supported and was produced by tightening the throat.

A great analogy for singing with an efficient straight tone is a kettle of popcorn. Imagine that the popping of the corn is the vibrato. If you cover the kettle with a lid, the popcorn won't be able to escape from the kettle. So if this were applied to singing, you must always be popping the corn, but you don't have to let it escape. When I sing with a straight tone, I think of it as *sitting* on the vibrato but never *stopping* the technique that creates it. In short, I'm always supporting my throat. When I allow for the reintroduction of vibrato, it sounds like a natural blossoming of my voice rather than a distracting explosion.

### EXERCISE 34: GO FROM STRAIGHT TONE TO SPINNING 1

- On a piano, an electronic keyboard, or a piano app, find and play the E below middle C (E3) if you are male or the E a third above middle C (E4) if you are female (see Figure 11 in the Appendix).
- Sing a straight-tone (not spinning) *ee* vowel on this note somewhat softly for ten seconds.
- Repeat the previous step, but this time gradually increase the volume until you are singing loudly.
- How does this feel? Does the voice feel a bit tight? Does a natural spin begin to occur?
- Repeat, but as you get louder, allow for a natural spin to begin to set the voice free. It is imperative that you support your throat as you increase the intensity of the vowel.

### EXERCISE 35: GO FROM STRAIGHT TONE TO SPINNING 2

- On a piano, an electronic keyboard, or a piano app, find and play the B below middle C (B3) if you are male or the B above middle C (B4) if you are female (see Figure 11 in the Appendix).
- In front of a mirror, sing an *ah* vowel with a straight tone on this note for ten seconds. Make sure you are supporting your throat.
- Repeat the previous step, but this time allow a vibrato to blossom in the sound after five seconds of straight tone.
- How does it feel? Is any part of your body shaking so that you can notice it in the mirror? If so, send the energy back to your support. The most common places I've seen an unsupported vibrato manifest itself are the neck, tongue, and jaw. The real work should be done below the throat, so that all you see is your jaw dropping and the tip of your tongue staying behind your bottom front teeth while the back of your tongue remains almost in contact with your upper back teeth.
- Repeat the previous steps until they feel comfortable and easeful.

## Dynamics

The word "dynamics" in music refers to volume and deliberate shifts in volume. Basic dynamics encompass the production of every sound from the softest (*pianissimo*) to the loudest (*fortissimo*). These include *piano* (soft), *mezzo piano* (medium soft), *mezzo forte* (medium loud), and *forte* (loud). *Crescendos* (soft to loud) and *decrescendos* (loud to soft) are effective basic tools of musical expression. Incorporating dynamics will bring more emotional life and dramatic specificity into your singing.

For example, what dynamics might you choose if you were singing a lullaby? Probably piano or pianissimo, right? What about a more complex song or scene? From an acting point of view, we could assign specific actions to certain dynamic shifts. We could say, "Try *not* to yell" when singing piano. Or how about "Let my inner light shine" when delivering a crescendo?

I referenced the song "Maria" in Chapter 1 (page 18). Tony is singing in an alleyway, putting himself in physical danger if he should be overheard and captured by the Puerto Rican gang members (the Sharks) who reside there. Yet he is compelled to pour out his heart through song and find his Maria. I imagine that he'd want to sing forte and fortissimo so that Maria would hear him but also that he is forcing himself to try to sing piano because he's in enemy territory. Therefore, the dynamic choices he chooses to employ give us a chance to *hear* his dramatic conflict, the one between action and obstacle, not just see it.

## EXERCISE 36: CRESCENDO AND DECRESCENDO

- On a piano, an electronic keyboard, or a piano app, find and play the E below middle C (E3) if you are male or the E a third above middle C (E4) if you are female (see Figure 11 in the Appendix).
- Sing an *ee* vowel on this note as quietly as possible (pianissimo), without adding any breathiness into your sound.
- Sustain this for ten seconds. If you can, allow a natural vibrato.
- Repeat the previous step, but sing the syllable as loudly as possible (fortissimo).
- Repeat, but this time begin singing pianissimo and allow the *ee* to slowly become louder (crescendo), growing to fortissimo.
- Repeat, but this time begin singing fortissimo, then gradually soften (decrescendo) to pianissimo.
- How does this feel? Are you engaging your support? Can you sustain an even, undisturbed vibrato when shifting your dynamics?
- What is happening with your jaw? Make sure not to close the jaw on the decrescendo. Dynamic variation is accomplished in

singing by *supporting* your throat and allowing the body to make subtle adjustments in air volume and pressure.

- Sing the syllable again, beginning with pianissimo, growing to a full fortissimo, then returning to pianissimo, all on one breath.
- Try this on other notes that you can comfortably sing. What do you feel? Are there certain notes that are easier that others when singing this exercise? Why?
- Keep repeating until you can accomplish this without straining in your throat. Think of employing a longer vocal tract, allowing more space in the pharynx. Nothing should be closing on any dynamic level or shift.

## Vocal range

Everyone with a physiologically undamaged throat has a complete vocal range that includes the chest voice, the middle voice, and the head voice. The exact pitches where the vocal registers lie differ from person to person. Each register is characterized by a difference in the length of the vocal cords, the position of the larynx, and the location of the resonators at play. In the chest, or lower, voice, the vocal cords are in a relaxed, neutral position. The larynx is low and vertical (untilted), and the dominant resonator is the chest. In the middle voice, or *passaggio* (Italian for "passageway"), the vocal cords begin to lengthen, the larynx slightly tilts toward the back, and the head resonators are used almost equally with the chest resonators.[2] In the head voice, the vocal cords have stretched and tightened, the larynx is maximally tilted, and the head resonators are dominant. The head voice should also contain *squillo*, a trumpet-like sound and resonance that gives high notes a metallic, shimmery quality.

[2] If you ever hear about someone singing in his or her *mix*, this means that the person is singing with a slightly narrowed vocal tract and a mix of the chest and head resonators, regardless of vocal register. This is very different from singing with a *voix mixte*, which is a *quasifalsetto* sound accomplished by backing off of the core vibration of the vocal cords and allowing more air into the actual sound (see page 68).

The head voice is not the same as *falsetto* singing in men. Falsetto singing is accomplished by singing from the edges of the vocal cords, thus eliminating core resonance, both in the head and in the chest, and vibration from your sound. You can't necessarily feel the edges of the cords, just an extreme lightness of sensation in the larynx. Falsetto is a useful tool for singing notes that are higher than you are capable of singing with a full sound. It can also be a great way to warm up and cool down the voice—if you are supporting it—because it's gentler on the vocal cords.

To envision your voice and its complete range, picture an hourglass: two rounded chambers connected by a narrow passageway. Now imagine setting the hourglass on its side. I prefer this image—a sideways orientation of the hourglass—because it eliminates the unhelpful perception that the voice is moving up and down. The two large chambers of the hourglass represent the chest and head registers of the voice, while the narrow area represents the middle voice, the *passaggio*.

## Chest voice

It's important that chest singing be very supported and simple. Even though your chest is the dominant resonator when you are singing in this register, there will still be some percentage of head voice in the sound. Your vocal onset, trajectory, and point of resonance must remain the same in *all* vocal registers.

### EXERCISE 37: FIND YOUR CHEST VOICE

- **Choose any monosyllabic word, such as "me," "hey," "hi," "whoa," or "who."**
- **Speak it slowly and fairly loudly.**
- **Is your jaw opening or dropping on the primary-vowel portion of the word? Remember to delay the diphthong until the very end of the word.**
- **Place your hand on your chest and experiment with opening and closing your jaw while saying any of these words. Does the chest**

vibrate more or less as the jaw opens? Make sure the vowel keeps moving away from the throat and out of the mouth as the jaw opens.

- Sing any or all of the above words on a comfortable chest note—a pitch where you would comfortably speak.
- Find a low-lying passage of your song and sing it. Can you sense the bright, communicative power of your chest voice? How does it feel to you?

## The *passaggio*

Navigating the middle voice, or *passaggio*, is what separates good singers from great singers. This area is full of physiological traps that can result in lots of tongue and throat tension, intonation problems, and nasality. Because the *passaggio* shares the resonances of the head and chest voices almost equally, it can be challenging to find a balance.

Classical singers often mistake a narrowing of the vocal tract with a covering over of the sound. This is an overrounding of vowels (especially *ah*) that will sound like a darkening of the vowel color. If this is accomplished by lowering the tongue and pulling the voice back and down, the voice will not have enough space and flexibility to freely sing high notes. A better solution is to allow the vowels to gather and slightly narrow, giving them increased height and depth, thus paving a smooth path to the head voice. Contemporary singers, on the other hand, often react to a perceived vocal restriction in the middle voice by spreading (see page 44). But spreading is not a substitute for a bright middle-voice sound, either.

Somewhere in the upper-middle part of your *passaggio*, you will reach a tipping point where closed vowels will require the same jaw space as open vowels. The gathering and focusing of vowels in the *passaggio* keeps the throat deep and flexible enough to allow you to transition into the head voice.

## EXERCISE 38: FIND YOUR *PASSAGGIO*

- On a piano, an electronic keyboard, or a piano app, find and play the E below middle C (E3) if you are male or the E above middle C (E4) if you are female (see Figure 11 in the Appendix).
- On this note, phonate an *ah* vowel in front of a mirror.
- Observe your lips, tongue, and jaw. Make sure there are two fingers of space between your upper and lower teeth.
- Repeat the previous steps, but this time move from the E up to the next note on the major scale (F sharp) and the note above that (G sharp), then back down again. You will be singing a simple major third (*do, re, mi, re, do*).
- On the highest note of this simple scale, do you feel something shift or change in your throat? Do you feel a buildup of pressure? Always make sure you are supporting.
- Sing the major-third scale again, but this time start a half step higher (i.e., on F) until you sense a subtle but distinct pressure and energy in the throat. You will know you have entered your *passaggio* because you'll have difficulty maintaining the vowel sound's integrity without widening your mouth and dropping your tongue toward the back of your throat. When you find the approximate note where this occurs, you have located the first note of your middle voice.
- Repeat the scale on the note where your *passaggio* begins and continue modulating up a half step five more times. Concentrate on making a specific *ah* sound, although your mouth shape should look like you're singing an *aw* vowel. Keep the tip of the tongue behind your bottom front teeth while the back of your tongue remains tall and disengaged. Always keep the lips in a soft pucker.

### EXERCISE 39: MAKE SPACE IN THE *PASSAGGIO* FOR VOWELS

- On a piano, an electronic keyboard, or a piano app, play a major-third scale beginning at your *passaggio* (see Exercise 38).
- Sing the scale on *ee*, making sure you have one finger of space between your top and bottom teeth.
- Repeat the previous step while modulating up by half steps.
- What do you observe? Keep repeating until it becomes almost impossible to sing the *ee* without resorting to the spreading and widening of the mouth. It is at *this* moment that you need more *vertical* space for the *ee* sound. This means that you need to practice singing closed vowels in your *middle passaggio* with two fingers of jaw space between your top and bottom teeth.
- Sing the scale again, but this time alternate between *ay* and *oo* vowel sounds.

## Head voice

As we sing notes that extend beyond the *passaggio*, we are using the *head voice*. The head voice relies on the resonators of the head (skull, cheeks, hard palate) to project sound. As with the chest voice, the head voice does not exclusively use one group of resonators; there should still be some chest resonance present in the head voice. With no chest resonance, the head voice will not sound connected to the other notes you sing. It may sound light, airy, and underpowered.

Ideally, your pharynx should be very round and expanded and your larynx should stay low when you sing high notes. This affords the voice enough space to exit the throat without our feeling the need to push, shout, and strain. Because the vocal cords are maximally stretching and vibrating at a higher frequency than they are in the chest voice, the throat will be emitting a great deal of energy. Therefore, everything we sing *before* singing in the upper register needs to have a stable foundation of support.

## EXERCISE 40: FIND YOUR HEAD VOICE

- Sing a major-third scale (*do, re, mi, re, do*) on *ah*, beginning on the note where you feel your *passaggio* starts (see Exercise 38). Continue modulating up by half steps.
- Inevitably, you will arrive at a note where you'll have difficulty sustaining a pure *ah* vowel. You will feel the *ah* becoming strangled. *This* note is the beginning of your head voice—your first high note. At this point, your vocal tract needs more height. Therefore, you need to find a color of *ah* that will be slightly darker and more "noble."
- Repeat the scale you sung in step 1, but this time sing it on an *aw* vowel. The *aw* is a darker, rounder version of *ah* that shares qualities of an open *oh* vowel (*oh* being darker than *ah*). Continue modulating up by half steps until, again, you run out of space. This will feel similar to the sensation of what happens at the upper end of your *passaggio*.
- How did this feel? Because head resonators can sound fairly bright, approaching them with a rounded sound adds depth and balance. In singing, we should always strive to find a balance between bright and dark sounds.

When we approach the very top notes of our natural vocal register, we need to efficiently use all the physiological space the body has to offer. Assuming we've been supporting and gathering our sound up to this point, where can we find this space? The simple answer is in the mouth. Picture a herd of horses trapped in a barn, tearing the place up, kicking the walls, and biting one another. How would you go about setting them free? You'd swing open the barn doors! The same applies to the extreme amount of energy required to sustain and *release* extreme high notes.

### EXERCISE 41: SMILE AT THE TOP

- Beginning with the first note of your head voice, sing a major-third scale, but only upward (i.e., *do, re, mi*—not *do, re, mi, re, do*) on *aw*.
- Modulate up by half steps until you encounter a note where you run out of space.
- When you encounter that note, drop your jaw so that there is more than two fingers of space between your upper and lower teeth *and* add a slight smile. In other words, pull your lips away from your teeth so that your front upper and lower teeth are exposed.
- How did this feel? If it doesn't feel like enough space, then repeat and open your jaw and lips until it does. At this point, you should look like you're about to bite into a very large apple.

## Belting

When it comes to style, I highly recommend you watch, listen, and practice as many examples as you can of whatever vocal style(s) at which you wish to excel. In this era of YouTube, you can watch nearly a century's worth of vocal performances in every style imaginable. I often tell people I have a master's degree in music from YouTube. That said, I would be derelict in my duty if I did not teach you a basic and *healthful* approach to the belting style of singing.

A belted sound contains a brightness and color that sounds to an audience as if the voice is using the power of chest resonance only. But a healthful belting technique cannot rely on chest resonance alone. To do so would lead to overinvolvement of and permanent damage to the throat. Inefficient belting (i.e., shouting) has shortened or ended countless promising careers before they could get off the ground. Therefore, you need to think of belting as a modification of *color* in the vocal technique I've mapped out for you.

If classical and contemporary singing can be defined as singing with a European accent, you should think of belting as singing with an American accent, complete with the wider, flatter, and brighter vowel sounds that come with it. When belting, your pharyngeal space needs to be a bit wider at the top than it is in other styles of singing. Picture a small slice of pizza hanging vertically by the crust. That is roughly the image you need to use in belting. The same general shape should also apply to your mouth. This will give you a slightly wider and brighter sound without your having to engage in spreading, which will pull up the larynx and add nasality.

Belting essentially boils down to the practice and sensation of one basic vowel sound: the *ae*, as in the words "back," "crack," and "lack." The *ae* is an open vowel sound, like *ah*, that contains the brightness of an *ee* sound. And, like the *ee*, it cannot be accurately phonated with the tongue in a low position. It's highly effective because it's both powerful and efficient.

## EXERCISE 42: FIND YOUR BELTING VOICE

- On a piano, an electronic keyboard, or a piano app, find and play the C an octave below middle C (C3) if you are male or middle C (C4) if you are female (see Figure 11 in the Appendix).
- Starting on that note, sing a major-fifth scale (*do, re, mi, fa, sol*) on the syllable *bae.* This should sound like the word "bad" without the final *d*. Make sure you sing a pure version of the vowel, with no hint of schwa (an *uh* sound).
- How does it feel? Can you feel that it's a bright, almost obnoxious sound?
- Sing the scale again, modulating up by half steps, until you encounter your *passaggio*.
- What do you observe? Can you sustain the sound without spreading? Observe your larynx—is it automatically popping up until a high position? It's vital that you follow the same rules of onset, support, and jaw space (see page 44) when singing with this sound.

- Sing the scale again, modulating up by half steps, until the voice feels like it can't sustain the vowel unless you add some air into the sound. Ideally, you should be able to sing a pure *ae* all the way up, through the *passaggio*, to the beginning of your head voice (also known as your *high belt*). Very rarely will you encounter repertoire that includes belted notes above an F. If you do, make sure you don't try to add *any* weight or power to the sound from the throat. Stick with the fundamental *ae* sounds and keep it flowing from over your cheeks.
- Choose a song that you feel should be sung in a belted style. Sing the entire song, but replace every syllable with the syllable *bae* (as in the word "bad" without the final *d*).
- How did this feel? Where could you feel your resonance? Could you successfully sustain the brightness of the sound without adding strain to the throat?
- Sing the entire song again, but this time put an element of the *ae* sound inside every vowel. In other words, sing all the words and their corresponding vowels, but send them through to the same physical place and position you felt on the pure *ae* sound.
- How did this feel? If you were able to successfully sustain and support the core brightness and power of the *ae* sound in your other vowels, you were probably belting!

# 3
# THE ARTIST PUTS IT ALL TOGETHER

I'd like to share with you my simple definition of what it means to be an artist. My experience leads me to the conclusion that great painters, sculptors, writers, and composers are often held in higher esteem as artists than performing artists are. Perhaps the saturation of mediocre performances in popular film, television, and music has contributed to a perception that performers aren't legitimate artists. If so, it is vital that we hold ourselves to a higher standard in the preparation and execution of our art. It should be our mission to remind the world that the greatest instrument of expression ever created is the human body. No canvas, piece of paper, or pattern of ink can ever be our equal *if* we give people the opportunity to see us at our perfectly imperfect, glorious best.

So what *is* an artist? I believe that an artist is *one who makes choices*. According to the eleventh edition of *Merriam-Webster's Collegiate Dictionary*, "choice" means "a number and variety to choose among" and "care in selecting."[1] As I have hoped to make clear in the previous pages, we as singers and actors want to develop an integrated process of making and executing choices.

Here's the rub: do you aspire to be a performing artist? Or are you simply a performer? To me, a performer is someone who strives to draw attention to himself. A performing artist, on the other hand, embraces the opportunity to participate in telling a story. A performer is interested only in telling a story about *herself* (how she sounds, looks, and feels). I think we'd all like to give great performances, but if narcissism is at the core of what you are pursuing, you'll never be a true artist. You may

---

[1] *Merriam-Webster's Collegiate Dictionary*, 11th ed., s.v. "choice."

even become successful, but I doubt you'll ever stir anyone's passions or transport anyone to another plane with your work. Plus, you'll never know what it feels like to let go and experience the blissful rush of trusting your true talent. Instead you'll exhaustively engage in a vain attempt to control everything. So for the aspiring performing artist reading this book, we will now explore approaches to the *art* of living through song.

## The chicken or the egg?

Fill in the blank in the following sentence:

The single most important component of a successful performance of a song is the _________.

A. Singing
B. Music
C. Text
D. Story

If you answered A, B, or C, you are missing the point of the entire enterprise. The singing, music, and text are all ingredients of a great performance, but they're meaningless if they don't weave together like a strand of DNA to tell a story that will move an audience.

If this were posited as a "which came first, the chicken or the egg" scenario in which the music is the chicken and the text is the egg, I'd pick the egg. A great composer understands how to use music to create drama, but the text is what gives it a specific story. So the text (as egg) is what gives birth to a living story in *action* (a chicken).

For example, let's say you are approaching a difficult passage of music while performing a song or an aria. If in that moment you are fairly unsure of what is going to come out of your throat and mouth—you're worried that you might wobble, crack, or miss a note—make sure that the *text* is communicated first and foremost. Don't attempt to linger and sustain a note or series of notes that are unstable, as this will remind the audience that you are having difficulty singing, thus distracting them from the story. Simply speak-sing the text and keep moving forward.

A great conductor I worked with compared watching auditions, which invariably require singers to perform difficult passages of music, to watching cars bottoming out in a pothole. He imagined himself sitting on his front porch watching cars encounter a huge pothole in the street that no one seems able to avoid. Eventually one car coasts along and cleanly navigates its way around the pothole. *This* is the singer whom the conductor hires.

In those circumstances, many singers opt for a sound they know they can sustain, even if it sounds *nothing* like the word they are singing. I don't employ this method because I don't believe in singing for the sake of making pretty sounds. *Great* singers rely on a technique that allows them to make any sound (especially vowels) intelligible on any note in their vocal ranges. And they accomplish this without modifying words. It's as simple as this: if it's unintelligible, it's not going to tell a story, period. Make it a goal that every word you speak or sing in a performance is heard and understood by your audience.

## Mastering legato

Has singing and acting simultaneously ever felt paradoxical, as if you are attempting two separate or even oppositional tasks? If so, you should explore the concept of legato (see page 34) as a way of binding your

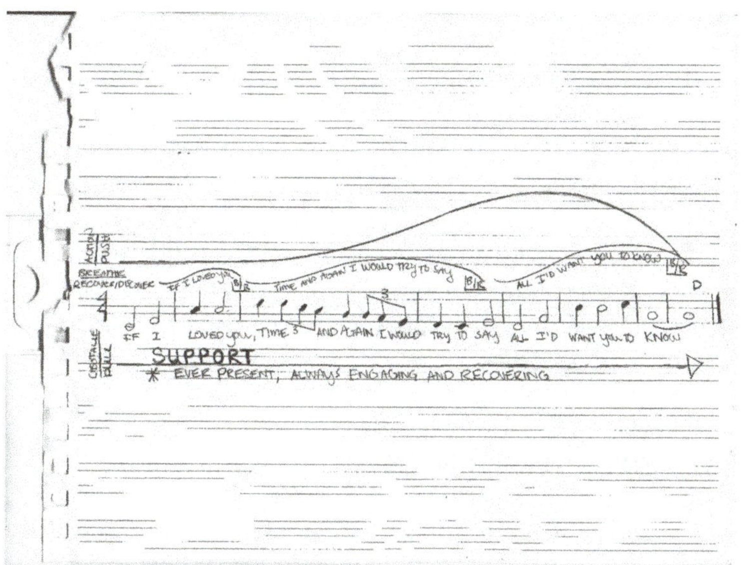


**Figure 10** Master legato chart.

musical phrases to your thoughts and fusing the music with the drama. In the chart in Figure 10, you will see that every musical concept has a yin–yang correlation in the discipline of acting. For example, a *phrase* of music is bound with a *thought* of text. And we can partner the act of *support* with the *obstacle*. Furthermore, you can see that focusing on macroscopic ideas and phrasing can free you from the prison of trying to "hit" individual notes and enunciate every word.

## Sinatra the storyteller

As a self-professed "Sinatraphile"—I've read at least four biographies of Frank Sinatra—I recall reading that watching Frank Sinatra perform a song is like watching a short film. This greatest of compliments revealed that Sinatra could tell a full, compelling story in a few short minutes. On *The Frank Sinatra Show* (*c.* 1957), Sinatra would often perform songs against the backdrop of simple theatrical sets. These were constructed with the intention of adding context and backstory to each song.

For example, he performed the Harold Arlen–Johnny Mercer masterpiece "One for My Baby (and One More for the Road)" in a tavern setting, complete with an actual bartender. Dressed in an overcoat and fedora, Sinatra sits and sings to the bartender, intermittently pulling on a cigarette that miraculously stays lit throughout the entire scene. He simply tells his story, without adding an overarching emotional color such as sadness or self-pity. It feels like the confession of a man struggling to accept his current plight. Because of the specificity of the setting and Sinatra's acting choices, we are transported beyond a mere performance and dropped into the middle of an honest story.

I can't speak to Mr. Sinatra's character offstage, but onstage he could be devastatingly truthful and authentic. He once said, "Whatever else has been said about me personally is unimportant. When I sing, I believe. I'm honest."

## The four moments

When I was studying at the University of Michigan, I learned a very important exercise from the late great teacher Gary Bird. For this and so much else, I owe Mr. Bird a huge debt of gratitude. In his classes, I came to believe for the first time that I was capable of great acting. Under his tutelage I was able to break free from self-consciousness and awaken my body.

Mr. Bird taught his students to identify four beats (see page 12) in every song and expand them into physical *moments.* These moments are characterized by a shift in the physical life of the character based on the actor's action and tactics choices. This means finding and building contrasts from beat to beat in *organic* movement, not *choreographed* movement.

***Moment 1: The prologue, or exposition***

**This is the moment when you, as the character, gather and discover information. We can call it the *What just happened* moment.**

***Moment 2: The development***

**This is when you process and make sense of the first moment. We'll call this the *I think THIS is what just happened* moment.**

***Moment 3: The climax***

**This is when the character has to decide what he or she is going to do with the information that has been discovered and processed. We can call this the *What am I going to DO about it* moment.**

***Moment 4: The epilogue, or resolution***

**This important and often unrealized moment is when the character has made a decision and has gained an awareness of the consequences of that decision. We'll call this the *THIS is what I'm going to do* moment.**

To use "If I Loved You" as an example, below is what my four moments might look like, based on my tactics-map exploration in Chapter 1 (see page 13). There are countless ways to shape our songs using the four moments, so this is just one example.

***Moment 1***

Tactic: to soften

But somehow I can see just exactly how I'd be

If I loved you, time and again I would try to say all I'd want you to know

If I loved you, words wouldn't come in an easy way. Round in circles I'd go

I'm imagining that Julie and I are standing face to face, on a diagonal, on stage right. I am standing to her left. Julie's back is facing the stage-right audience. I begin moment 1 by looking her in the eye on "But somehow I can see," then slowly walking four or five steps backwards on a diagonal (up and stage left) on "just exactly how I'd be." I stop moving so I can sing to Julie, "If I loved you, time and again I would try to say all I'd want you to know." Then I flatten my body angle so I face the audience and sing, "If I loved you, words wouldn't come in an easy way. Round in circles I'd go." My moment 1 physical choices are very still and calm, based on my tactic, to soften. The audience should be very focused on my eyes at this point.

***Moment 2***

Tactic: to confess

Longing to tell you, but afraid and shy,

I'd let my golden chances pass me by

This moment happens quickly. I'm going to abruptly turn my body and face the stage-left audience because I don't want Julie to read my discomfort and vulnerability. I'm also trying to suppress elements of anger (at the feelings of discomfort) building inside me in this moment, which I can play in my breath and body. Specifically, it should look like I'm struggling to hold it together.

***Moment 3***

Tactic: to threaten

Soon you'd leave me

Off you would go in the midst of day

Never, never to know how I loved you

I will turn to face Julie (who is still downstage right) on "Soon you'd leave me, off you would go in the midst of day, never, never to know." This will read like a strong physical accusation and warning. This will also be the largest, most explosive physical moment of the scene. Ideally, the audience should feel (momentarily) that Julie *could* be in physical danger. I'm not going to go too far with this, because the obstacle will temper my physicality. The obstacle in this moment is my realization of Julie's innocence and physical fragility in comparison to mine. I'll cross diagonally from upstage left, where I'm standing, toward Julie on "How I loved you." Again, this cross should be physically strong. Maybe my physical intention is to grab and shake her, but I'm going to play the *conflict* of my threaten tactic with a discovery of her innocence. Perhaps I see a look of terror on her face, which stops me in my tracks.

***Moment 4***
Tactic: to recover
If I loved you.

I will use this moment to attempt to "catch my breath," both literally and figuratively. I feel that one of Billy's self-defense mechanisms is "playing it cool," which I'll play. Clearly this recovery shouldn't look or be easy, because the previous moment was the opposite of playing it cool. Physically, the audience should see me settle into a somewhat casual posture or physicality, but perhaps I'm now unable to sustain eye contact with Julie.

Can you see how I took my cues from the earlier dramatic analysis of "If I Loved You" to build and block the song as a scene? I didn't choreograph movements beyond walking and shifting focus, but I made room for specific spontaneous gestures and movements to occur. If you really commit to the tactics you choose to play, your talent will take over, manifesting itself in a compelling and truthful physicality.

## EXERCISE 43: IDENTIFY THE FOUR MOMENTS

- **Reopen your notebook to the place where you handwrote your song lyrics.**

- Go through the text of your song and roughly determine where you feel the four moments occur.
- Consider what is happening in these moments as information transmitted by the composer and lyricist. Where does it seem that the music is building? Is there a climactic moment, musically? Is there a resolution or denouement?
- Now, on your feet, determine a simple blocking, or series of movements, for the song, based on these four moments. You will essentially be directing your own performance. Each moment should occur in a specific spot on the stage and have its own physical life. Make sure to
  - experiment with stillness in one moment and explosion in another;
  - include a lateral or diagonal movement; and
  - include a movement directly downstage, toward the audience.
- Postpone moment 4 for as long as possible. The audience will be with you on this journey, so live in the problem—the action and obstacle. If you reach a dramatic conclusion too early, you'll have nothing left to play.
- Put the four moments together and perform your song. How does it feel? Do you feel a sense of physical freedom? Is your performance specific? Is there a natural buildup to the climactic moment (moment 3) of your song?

## Ancillary actions

During most auditions, and even during some performances, there are only minimal props and sets at our disposal. Usually these will include nothing more than a stool or chair, music stand, and piano. But I'm a big proponent of using these tools to the fullest extent possible. All these objects afford you opportunities to physically relate to your performance space. More important, they give you something tangible to *do*. Performing physical tasks, such as sitting in a chair, are what I call *ancillary actions*. These are defined as literal things you can do secondarily *in support* of your primary action. Acting is about doing, not feeling, so ancillary actions are another way to take the focus off yourself.

In life, we are always looking for ways to alleviate feelings of self-consciousness in social situations. For example, if you were to attend a cocktail party this evening, what's the first thing you'd want to do? My guess is that you'd make a beeline for the bar or buffet. Why? Because you know that sipping a drink or holding a plate of food will make you feel more comfortable when you begin conversations with the other guests.

The same concept applies to performing. Have you ever sung with a handheld microphone? Did it give you a sense of physical freedom or of being grounded? Maybe you've performed behind a music stand and discovered that grabbing onto it helped you feel more centered. Standing behind a chair and leaning on it with your hands could be a useful way of approaching a scene about a negotiation or confession. Sitting on a stool next to a piano could signal that the action takes place in a bar. Also, sitting on something gives you a different vertical plane to play, provided that you include moments of standing. Once, I even sat on top of a piano while playing a character I decided was drunk with love. These examples of ancillary actions can help you build detailed, physically free performances.

## EXERCISE 44: PERFORM ANCILLARY ACTIONS

- **Place a chair in the middle of a large room.**
- **Stand directly behind the chair, imagining that your audience is in front of the chair.**
- **What do you observe and feel? Do you instinctively want to put your hands on the back of the chair or lean on it?**

- **Make a physical choice to use the chair. Lean on it; sit on it; stand on it; put a foot on it.**
- **Repeat, and sing the first *moment* (beat) of your song.**
- **How did this feel? Did the architecture of the chair help you feel more connected to the space? Could it make the scene you are playing more *specific*?**

## Magical objects

Objects and props, both real or imaginary, have substantial creative potential. What do magic wands represent in the Harry Potter films, for example? When Harry grasps his wand, we as an audience expect something magical or spectacular to happen. The same thing goes for straight razors in *Sweeney Todd*. In the song "My Friends," Sweeney becomes reacquainted with his deadly "tools," vowing that they will soon drip "rubies" in his plot for bloody revenge. He finishes the song proclaiming, "My right hand is complete again!" while thrusting his razor upward in anticipation.

In context, Sweeney's razor is a powerful object, capable of terrible violence. But straight razors can be found in most local barber shops even today. And when folded up, they seem perfectly innocuous and ordinary. It's the power bestowed upon them by the story, and the performer's wielding of them, that make them such effective dramatic tools. In the hands of an imaginative actor, any object can become a theatrically magical object.

### EXERCISE 45: USE A MAGICAL OBJECT

- **Pick up a pen and observe its size and shape. Make a list of the objects it could represent. A knife? The handle of a whip? A magic wand?**

- Choose to imagine that the pen is one of these objects. Imagine the weight, the shape, and the power of the object.
- What do you observe and feel when you do this?
- Sing your song while handling the pen, pretending that it is the object of your choice. Don't worry if it doesn't make literal sense with your scene.
- Choose moments when you will focus on the object and juxtapose them with moments when you will focus on your scene partner.
- Did this make you feel self-conscious? If so, repeat until you truly enjoy including the object in the song.
- Write down three potential *imaginary* objects that you could handle while singing your song. Which of the three are you most compelled to use?
- Choose one and imagine picking it up, holding it, and using it. Again, commit to sensing its weight, size, and shape. If you are specific in your handling and miming of the object, the audience will see it, too!
- Sing your entire song again, while using the *imagined* object as you see fit. Try to allow yourself the freedom to play with the object without predetermining how you use it.
- How did this feel? Were you able to see and feel the object in your imagination?

## The visceral power of music

When performing a song, you almost always have a wonderful and potent partner: the music. In fact, music can be so powerful that sometimes I watch a film with the volume turned down, and I often hit the mute button during scary movies. Remember the expression "Cue the violins"? Film sound tracks are vital tools that filmmakers employ to evoke strong feelings in the viewer. Can you imagine watching the opening of *Star Wars* without the brilliant fanfare, composed by John Williams?

In order to completely appreciate the role of the music in the song you have chosen to sing, you should obtain a prerecorded accompaniment that you can use while practicing at home. These audio files, called backing tracks, are available online. High-quality sources include MusicNotes.com and SheetMusicPlus.com. Usually these consist of a piano or synthesized piano playing the song without the melody line. Alternatively, you could record a friend or teacher playing the song and use that in your practice.

## EXERCISE 46: LISTEN TO THE MUSIC

- Play a recording of the accompaniment to your song. Sit down and listen with your eyes closed. What are your impressions of the music?
- Play the backing track again, then write down what you hear in your notebook. Is the music painting a picture for you? Does it suggest a specific setting or place? What emotions does the music evoke in you? Does it make you feel sad, excited, bittersweet? If you described them in colors, what would they be? Write down everything that crosses your mind.
- Does the music paint a picture in your mind of a place or specific setting? If, so write it down in detail.
- Looking at everything you've written down in this exercise, can you determine how the music fits with the story you are telling? How does it apply to the four moments exercise? Does it change any of the action or beat choices you had previously made? Does listening and understanding the power of the music alone help you to appreciate the assistance being provided to you by the composer?

In Chapter 1, we learned about going to the zero (see page 24). This concept is based in my firm belief that a living, breathing human being is fundamentally and intrinsically interesting to an audience. When applying this concept to living through song, we need to deepen our trust in the music. It's as if you are standing in front of a blank canvas that the composer immediately paints into a rich, living backdrop. The music can evoke an emotional life and stir an audience's imagination without your having to do anything. And every single person in the audience will react to the music differently. This is all possible if you trust the music. Resist the temptation to *show* the audience how they *should* feel. Always play specific *actions*, not emotions, especially when living through song.

## EXERCISE 47: LET THE MUSIC BE A BLANK CANVAS

- Invite a friend to help you with this exercise.
- Put on the prerecorded accompaniment to your song.
- As your friend watches you, stand still in the center of your room or playing space, then make eye contact with your imaginary scene partner. Do your best to go to the zero, applying the techniques covered in Chapter 1 (page 24).
- Ask your friend to tell you what she thought the song was about. What setting and emotions did she hear in the music? Did she think you were playing a specific story or emotion(s)?
- Were you surprised at what your friend observed or felt? Was it different from what you wrote down about the music in Exercise 46?
- What was instructive about your friend's observations, and how might they affect your performance of the song?
- This exercise will only work if you commit to it. If your friend detects you dropping focus or concentration, she will be too distracted to feel or observe much beyond your self-consciousness.

- Ask your friend to switch places with you and perform the same exercise. Imagine that you are an audience member who wants to believe that she is telling a story. What might the story be? How would you describe the emotional life of the character?
- Were you surprised at what you saw and heard? Would it change the way you interpret and perform your song? Write down everything you observe.

## Don't put the swing in the swing

Frank Sinatra had many nicknames and monikers, including the King of Swing. What I find instructive about this is that Sinatra's delivery of swing didn't really swing at all. He would never panic or let the music pull him forward out of his delivery. Instead he would tease the rhythm, forever slowing down then speeding up in a charming game of musical cat and mouse. In other words, he never put the swing in the swing.

I think Sinatra had an innate understanding of the power of *opposites*. And when we apply this dramatic concept to music, we find balance. To maximize the power of the music, make a dramatic choice that's oppositional to the tempo. In other words, find the push–pull.

### EXERCISE 48: FIND THE OPPOSITES

- Play the prerecorded accompaniment to your song. What do you observe about its tempo? Is it fast or slow? Does it have a walking pace? What does it remind you of? Could you dance to it? What is the style of the piece? Write down at least five descriptions of the tempo.
- Play the accompaniment again. Move your arms to the music, as if you are conducting the song. How did this feel? Do you begin to sense the internal rhythm of the song physically?

- **Play the accompaniment again, but this time sing the song while moving your arms and body to the beat. How did you feel? This is a way of physicalizing the action scene but is missing a key component: the *obstacle*. Without an obstacle, you will put the swing in the swing!**
- **Play the accompaniment again, but this time sing the song while exploring physical *opposition* to the rhythm. If the song is slow, find moments of physical urgency. Conversely, if it's fast, make smooth and calm movements. How did this feel? Repeat until it feels like you're paddling a kayak upriver against the flow of the water. *This* is the ideal, oppositional approach to finding a dramatic push–pull balance in the music.**

## Don't beat time with your voice

Just as you find dramatic balance in the music, it is imperative that you do so in your voice. Your phrases—sung in the "language" of *legato* (see page 34)—must be greater and longer than each individual note and measure of music. If you are emphasizing every downbeat (the first note of every measure), the audience will be reminded that you are performing a song—not living through song. You might as well invite them to clap along as though you're all participating in a rollicking drinking song. Rather, aim to combine the character's thought with a *phrase* of music. This keeps you from beating time, or conducting, with your voice.

### EXERCISE 49: SING IN COMPLETE THOUGHTS

- **Sing your song with the prerecorded accompaniment. Strictly observe the time signature (4/4, 3/4, or whatever it is), and purposely emphasize every downbeat vocally.**

- **How did this feel? Did your voice feel free? How did this affect your breathing? How often did you have to take a breath? Did you feel that you were communicating the story?**
- **Look at the lyrics of your song in your notebook. Decide where you think complete thoughts occur and write a large check mark beside every new thought.**
- **Sing your song again, but this time breathe only where you decide the thoughts occur. (If a complete thought is so long that you need to take a breath within it, go ahead, but make sure you reengage your support each time [see page 48].)**
- **Don't emphasize the words on the downbeats unless that makes sense in communicating a thought.**
- **How did this feel? Were you able to support and complete the thoughts on one breath? Did the song feel more connected than it did when you were emphasizing every downbeat?**

## Emphasize selectively

When we sing, just as when we perform a classical text, we can be tempted to emphasize too many syllables or sounds. This is born from the desire to communicate and enunciate. When it comes to singing, perhaps we think that just because a musical note changes, we have to emphasize it each time. But a change in pitch does not necessarily demand that we call attention to it. Such repeated emphasis forces the audience to hear and process too many sounds, which makes it difficult to follow or tune in to your story.

I like to follow a simple rule that I use when performing Shakespeare. I look for the operative words and syllables that match the *thought* of each sentence and rarely emphasize more than two words per sentence. This allows you to tell the story via the *thoughts* of the sentence instead of bash the audience over the head with every word.

Think of Hamlet's famous line "To be or not to be." This is the first line of a soliloquy in which Hamlet contemplates suicide. The novice

Shakespearean interpreter might land the text like this: *TO BE or NOT TO BE*. But the experienced Shakespearean interpreter might emphasize fewer words. He might say, *To BE… or NOT to be.* Or he might say, *To BE or not… to BE.* Each difference in emphasis offers a unique interpretation of the phrase and, by extension, the character's action and intention.

It's the same when you're singing a phrase of music. In addition, being selective about where you put your emphasis saves energy by keeping your airflow uninterrupted. This will allow you to sing longer and more fully on every phrase.

## EXERCISE 50: CHOOSE WHAT TO EMPHASIZE

- Choose the two most important and operative words of the first sentence or phrase of your song.
- Sing the phrase or sentence, emphasizing the two words you selected *and* their corresponding musical notes. Make sure the other notes or words are still moving forward toward the peak of your legato line and thought. Singing still requires more energy and urgency than speech!
- How did this feel? Could you match the thought with your breath?
- Review the entire text of your song and choose two words to emphasize in every sentence or phrase.
- Sing the entire song, putting an emphasis on the words you chose.
- How did this feel? Were you able to make your points more clearly? How did this affect your ability to sing? Was it harder or easier?

## Surf the waves

Imagine every phrase of music you sing resembling a great wave as it builds up, curls, and crashes. You know that waves are made up of millions of tiny droplets of water, but when their energy comes together as a wave, all we perceive is the motion. Similarly, a page of music consists of individual notes, but these discrete symbols are merely a starting point. In singing and transcending the music, we need to play a game of connect the dots and bind these notes together into a connected *wave of sound*.

## EXERCISE 51: IDENTIFY THE WAVES

- Sing the first musical phrase of your song (the melody with the lyrics). If it were a wave, where would it crest? Draw a wave over the lyrics, indicating the crest of the music.
- Repeat the previous step for every phrase of your song. Do the musical crests logically correspond to the crests of the text—i.e., the syllable of the word that lands your thought or makes your point?
- Try lining up the emphasis point of the thought (as expressed in the lyrics) with the cresting of the musical wave.
- Sing the entire song, with the lyrics, fully committing to the waves of the music.
- How did this feel? Did it feel connected and musical? Can you allow yourself to release your breath and vocal energy to the wave of sound? Repeat until you feel yourself letting go of trying to control your voice.

## The mime and the statue

If you were unable to utter a single sound, would it be possible for you to tell a story through song, using your movements alone? Conversely, if you were wrapped in a mummy costume and unable to move, could you sing your story that way?

The "three circles" concept we explored in Chapter 1 (page 25)—the notion of underplaying and overplaying your action in a scene, then finding the middle ground between the two—is especially useful when your lines are set to music, as they are in song. This is because we are often seduced by the music into *competing* with it. To find the middle ground, I like to imagine myself at extremes—as an expressive, rubber-limbed mime who conveys every thought with a gesture and as a marble statue who can't move even if he wanted to.

For those of you who have developed certain habits of movement, try keeping yourself still. In these moments of stillness, channel your physical energy into your singing, and truthful movement will blossom outward from there. For those of you who feel self-conscious or doubt your physical abilities as an actor, pretend to be a mime. If you commit to your choice, you may experience a physical awakening. There are no right or wrong ways to do this, but without fully committing to and playing with these concepts, you will only reinforce your old habits. So risk doing it "wrong."

## EXERCISE 52: EXPLORE MOVEMENT AND STILLNESS

- Imagine that you are mute. Play the prerecorded accompaniment to your song and act out the story for an imaginary audience using only your body.
- How did this feel? Did you have a strong sense of physical activation?
- Repeat the first step, but this time act out the story for an imaginary partner.
- Did you feel physically free and activated? Were your movements *specific*?
- Now imagine that you are completely physically immobilized. Stand with your hands at your sides, and—except for your jaw, eyelids, and breathing—do not move a muscle. You are a *statue*. Stand like this for three minutes.
- Repeat the previous step while playing the prerecorded accompaniment to your song. Imagine you are singing the piece, but don't. Breathe where you would ordinarily breathe.

- **Is this difficult to do? Were you tempted to move, shift your weight, or fidget?**
- **While pretending that you are a statue, play the accompaniment to your song, but this time sing along with it. Funnel all your energy into your singing voice, but don't make any additional movements. Again, make sure you support your voice from the diaphragm.**
- **How did this feel? Did your voice feel stronger or more focused?**

## Repetition is the soul of art

A closing thought I'd like to leave you with is a core mantra I continually repeat to my students: "repetition is the soul of art." Another way of saying this is practice makes permanent.

I studied acting in graduate school with Jon Jory, who has enjoyed a historic career as a director, playwright, and teacher. Mr. Jory had a profound impact on my development as an actor. His approach was always practical and based on making and trying out choices. He would often say that "ideas are cheap." He meant that the creative process can include a nearly infinite number of variations and choices when you're playing a character or scene. In working a beat, he'd often say, "Do it again, but make it different." He once made me repeat a line fifteen times in a row, but this nerve-racking experience was an epiphany for me. I was surprised and amazed as I found a spontaneous way to do that one single thing differently again and again and again.

I cannot stress to you enough the value of repetition as you apply the lessons and exercises in this book. This is different than practicing the same exact choice over and over again. That's equivalent to the definition on insanity (doing the same thing and expecting different results). Instead, repeat the process of trial and error. This will invariably lead to many failures and feelings of frustration, but that is a central component the learning process. Trial and error is the way a true performing artist measures their growth on a long, beautiful journey.

# APPENDIX

I've decided to include some exercises that you might find helpful in both warming up and warming down for your auditions, classes, lessons, and performances.

Throughout the book I've referred to certain notes on a piano. Figure 11, the keyboard diagram, should make very clear and simple how to decipher the notes I've described.

I'll begin my first exercise by helping you check in with the relationship between your mind and your feelings. *Centering* yourself is vital if you want to feel like you can breathe and have a clear head before you set foot onstage. You might find this challenging because your attempts to warm up have mostly been based on external physical activity. So, let's explore a warm up that focuses on what's going on in your *true* center: the thoughts and feelings in your brain and how they connect to your body and its senses.

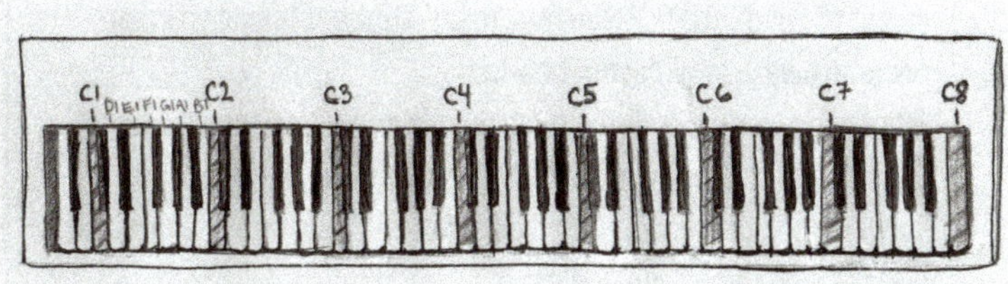


**Figure 11** Keyboard diagram.

## EXERCISE A: CHECKING IN WITH YOUR THOUGHTS, SENSES, AND FEELINGS

- Find a thick book, approximately two inches wide.
- Place the book on a clean floor, with enough space for you to lie down.
- Lie down on your back, placing the book under the back of your head like a pillow. This will create a gentle stretching of your neck and spine.
- Let your eyelids fall closed. Allow air to be inhaled through your nose and out through your mouth. See if you can also allow your jaw to fall open. Stay in this state with your eyes and your breathing throughout this exercise.
- How does your body *feel?* Can you feel the gravity pulling you closer to the floor? Are you physically holding on to anything in your body? Limb by limb, allow everything to get heavier. Are you tired? Are you sore anywhere? Are you hot or cold? Are you hungry or thirsty? Can you sense your own heartbeat? See how many things you can make yourself aware of with your body.
- What do you *hear*? What does your breathing sound like? Are there other sounds in the room? Can you hear sounds from another room or hallway? What can you hear outside? Is there the sound of wind? Traffic? See how many different things you can become aware of with your hearing.
- What can you *smell*? What does the air around you smell like? Can you smell your own clothes or breath? Can you detect the smell of food or cooking from your kitchen? How many different and detailed things can you smell?
- What can you taste? Did you eat something before you began this exercise? If so, can you still taste anything? Did you have

something to drink? Can you taste toothpaste or mouthwash? See how many different things you can taste.

- *How* do you feel? Try to analyze your emotions. Are you feeling nervous about anything? Concerned or doubtful? Confident? Excited? Emotions are neither good nor bad, but rarely do we take the time to acknowledge them. Do your best to be *honest* about how many emotions you are currently feeling. What could be useful about naming these emotions? Could any of them be useful to you in playing a character? Does naming your feelings make it easier for you to breathe and let go of anything?
- Slowly allow your eyes to open. What do you see? What is the pattern on the ceiling? What color is it? Slightly allow your head to move and scan the room. What else do you see? How many *details* do you observe with the objects in the room. What is the quality of the light? Is it daytime or nighttime?

Thoroughly observe as many things as possible.

- As slowly as possible, return to a position of standing. What's different about how you feel versus how you felt before you performed the exercise?

The next exercise is a very simple vocal warm up that you can perform in approximately 20 minutes.

It includes the basic concepts covered in Chapter 2 of this book. If you don't have access to a piano, there are many keyboard apps available that you can download onto your phone. I've personally practiced this warm up on my local subway platform, using only my phone and a set of ear buds.

## EXERCISE B: A SIMPLE VOCAL WARM UP

*A gentle sigh*

- With teeth and mouth closed, keep the tip of the tongue in contact with the lower teeth/gums. Keep the middle part of the tongue in contact with the back portion of the hard palate.
- Begin with a free, unstructured and gentle phonation by softly sighing through the nose. Allow the voice to lightly travel through different pitches, high to low and low to high.
- Gently and softly hum a simple song like *Mary Had a Little Lamb* or *Happy Birthday*.
- Make sure you are humming through the nose with your mouth closed.
- Keep the larynx from moving upward at the vocal onset (avoid a glottal attack).
- Activate the pharynx (and not the tongue) to form vowels.
- Slowly drop the jaw while humming an *ng* sound (as in the final sound of the word *goiNG*).
- Keep the air and sound exiting through the nose.
- Hum a simple three-note-scale on *ng* (1-2-3-2-1). Begin at *C4* (for men) or *C5* (for women).
- Modulate up twelve times, by half steps.
- Repeat, humming a five-note descending scale (5-4-3-2-1) at *F5* (for men) or *F6* (for women).
- Modulate eight times by half steps.
- Drop the jaw beginning on *ng* and open to a singing an *ee* vowel. Do this on either *E4* or *E5*. Try to feel the *ee* vibrating in the cheek bones. Let the pharynx (the back of the mouth/throat) make the vowel, instead of the muscular engagement of the tongue.
- Repeat, but now begin singing *ee* for approximately ten seconds. Recover your support and sing *ee-oo-ee-oo-ee-oo-ee-oo-ee-oo*. Look to keep both vowels in the same resonance (the *ee* gives the *oo* brightness, the *oo* keeps the *ee* rounded and focused).

- Using a mirror, try to keep the tongue tall and unactivated (flexed). Replace the tongue with the dropping of the jaw.
- Sing five-note major scales (1,2,3,4,5,4,3,2,1) on either *C3* or *C4.* Experiment with vowel combinations of *ee eh ah oh* and *oo*. Mix them up, find different combinations of the vowels.
- Modulate by half steps twelve times.

*Stillness and motion*

- In 6/8 time (like a drinking song) sing an arpeggio combination of 1,3,5,3,1 (*do, mi, so, mi, do*).
- Begin on either *C3* or *C4.* Start with the *ah* vowel. Like the previous exercise, play with different vowels (and combinations of vowels).
- Modulate by half steps twelve times.
- Alternate between stillness and movement on every modulation.

*Portamento*

- Beginning at *C3* or *C4* slide/allow the voice to span an octave (to *C4* or *C5*) on one vowel. *Allow* the voice to move without "placing" the notes. This is called a portamento or "carriage" of the voice.
- If you can, perform this exercise with the use of *vibrato* to move the voice from pitch to pitch. It may feel or sound like you are scooping or sliding your voice.
- Modulate twelve times via half steps.

*Articulation*

- Pick tongue twisters i.e., "lips teeth tip of the tongue, split the split pea soup, please" or "she sells sea shells by the sea shore."
- Sing the line on one note, beginning on *C3* or *C4.*

- Try to find the balance between articulation and legato. The line should be completely intelligible but not choppy.
- Don't let the consonants dictate/interrupt the airflow.
- Modulate by half steps twelve times.

The practice of warming up is vital to giving a consistent, healthy performance, but often the importance of *warming down* is overlooked.

## EXERCISE C: WARMING UP AND DOWN WITH A CUP AND A STRAW

- Pour water into a water glass, filling it half-way.
- Find a basic drinking straw. Make sure the straw is longer than the glass.
- Insert the bottom of the straw into the glass, just below the water level.
- Gently begin blowing bubbles in the water. Make sure the flow of the bubbles is even and not erratic. Also, be sure there are not water "volcanos" exploding out of the glass. No water should escape the glass.
- Add phonation of a gentle hum to the blowing of air through the straw. Again, see if you can keep the surface bubbles in the glass consistent.
- Continue but add vocal variation. Slide the voice from low notes to higher notes, then back again. Make sure not to add volume to get to the higher notes. Can you keep the airflow consistent without disrupting the bubbles?
- Perform this exercise whenever possible, especially when you feel fatigued from singing or speaking.

I'm going to follow-up on this simple warm up/warm down with an exceptionally practical method of awaking your support and breathing. I've covered the importance of supporting at length in Chapter 2 and here is another way to practice it.

## EXERCISE D: AWAKEN YOUR SUPPORT WITH A BALLOON

- Purchase a bag of simple party balloons.
- Take out a single balloon and fill it using your own lips and breath.
- What do you notice about your breathing? How is your breathing different from your normal, everyday way of breathing?
- Begin blowing up another balloon. This time pay close attention to your ribs and the *expansion* of your thoracic cavity. Can or do you feel how it continues to push outward as you fill the balloon? Can you replicate this breathing and support from the outward movement of the ribs and thoracic cavity (diaphragm) while exhaling *without* the balloon?
- Fill several more balloons until the breathing and outward movement of your ribs and abdomen (support) begin to feel easy to engage.

In Chapter 1 I discuss the concept of targeting. By this I mean exploring and deciding who your scene partner is when acting and taking into consideration the audience. The following exercise is designed to help you physically direct your energy and intentions through a specific physical action. It will also incorporate an element of rhythm.

## EXERCISE E: TARGETING, INTENTION, AND RHYTHM

- Find a tennis ball that still has a lot of life and bounce left in it
- Locate a room with minimal furniture, preferably a rehearsal room or dance space. Make sure there is nothing hanging on the walls, like picture frames, etc.

- Practice throwing the tennis ball against the wall. Can you stand at a distance that allows the ball to bounce once on the floor as it ricochets back to you? Continue this action until you can consistently throw it and catch the tennis ball (off one bounce) in a steady, predictable rhythm.
- Observe your breathing—are you holding your breath? Practice allowing your body to breathe with more fluidity, breathing *all* the air out of your lungs on every exhalation.
- Observe your body, specifically your neck and spine. How does your body feel? Do you feel a bit tight and muscular? Is the back of your neck shortened or pinched? See if you can allow your neck, spine, and body to lengthen and release, as if your head is dangling from a string.
- Decide that your scene partner is standing exactly where you are throwing the tennis ball (the target). Choose a line of text and throw the tennis ball at the target (which is now your imaginary scene partner) on the operative or stress word of the sentence. For instance, if the line was "and I can't stand him!" I would throw the ball on the word *stand.* "And I can't *stand* him."
- Repeat ten times. How did this feel? Does your body feel activated and engaged?
- Decide to include an imaginary audience into the action. What if there were one thousand people seated behind your target? Repeat throwing the ball at your target, including text ten more times. How did this affect the volume and size of your voice? Did your physicality and posture feel more expansive?
- Experiment with imagining your audience moving to other locations around you and your target. What if the audience surrounded you? What if it was located only on the left and right sides of your body like a runway? Repeat throwing the ball at your target, speaking your text ten more times. Did this change

**anything physically about the way you delivered your text? Did your body feel different?**

- **Repeat the exercise ten more times. Purposely and willfully try to change your intention and the way you say your line. Do you notice that there can be specific ways to adjust your intentions, even when the physical action and text remains the same? It is important that you recognize the amount of freedom you have, even within a fixed structure (space, text, blocking).**

We began this section with an exercise that focused on an inside-out approach to warming up. By this, I mean starting with a calm, deliberate practice of performing tasks with conscious thought. Outside-in approaches can be very useful and effective, especially in warming up and warming down our bodies. But as performing *artists* I strongly feel that our artistic *process* must come from our deepest, quietest, and most personal place. For me, this requires that everything I do when acting and singing must come from my heart and soul. I'm going to close things out with two exercises that have been vital to my growth and success as an artist. Let's explore some approaches to addressing what you *want* to believe about your talent, ability, and potential versus what you subconsciously *might* believe about your limitations.

## EXERCISE F: ADDRESSING THE SUBCONSCIOUS

- **Get a notebook and write down at least three of your biggest fears about your ability as a performer. Make sure to address one fear as it relates to singing, and another as it relates to acting.**

- What did you write? Would it be possible to rewrite your fear into something positive? For example, if you wrote "I don't think I'll ever learn to sing," what if you substituted it with "Today, I'm committed to becoming a better singer." What we are doing is pulling our subconscious beliefs and fears out of the darkness and consciously addressing them. Like it or not, no subconscious will believe whatever you tell it. The story of your life is etched in your subconscious and it often can result in you sabotaging yourself when you begin pushing beyond your comfort zone. It's like a hard drive on a computer. The good news is that it's not permanently wired into your brain—you can consciously replace the thoughts and beliefs in the subconscious. Scientifically, it's called *neurolinguistic programming*, but we more commonly can call these *affirmations.* Affirmations work, but most people don't really understand how and why they work. If you spent every day reciting an affirmation in the mirror five times, you probably won't make a big impact in really penetrating your subconscious. This is because you've been practicing your subconscious beliefs for most of your life. Do you really think you can replace those thoughts by saying something to yourself five times? The issue is repetition.
- Pick one of the positive responses you wrote in response to one of your fears. Set a timer for five minutes and recite the line, out loud, for five minutes. Make sure you are speaking the line with deliberate purpose and belief. How did this feel to you? Was it challenging to say the same thing that many times over the course of five minutes? Does the statement you repeated feel more truthful than it did before you started the exercise?
- Pick another response that you wrote in response to another fear. In front of a mirror, recite the line to yourself, out loud, for five minutes. Don't allow yourself to become distracted by your

appearance. Continue speaking the line, with purpose and truth with your eyes. How did this feel? Did it feel like the five minutes were never going to end? Did you sense discomfort? Most likely this is challenging because your subconscious doesn't want to change and is putting up a fight.

- Continue this practice, once a day for a week. See if you can increase your stamina and ability to recite the same positive affirmation that *you* wrote for up to 15 minutes at a time. After a week, ask yourself if the new belief has become more powerful than your older subconscious belief.

A final impediment to creating a successful performance might be that you've never taken the time to imagine what it would look and *feel* like beforehand. If you can really see yourself succeeding in your mind's eye, then you've created a much stronger possibility of it actually happening.

## EXERCISE G: THE POWER OF VISUALIZATION

- In your notebook, write down how you would ideally like to feel *during* and *after* a specific performance. It can be anything from an audition, a class, a private lesson, or a live performance with an audience. Choose a specific song or sustained moment that you might find intimidating, the *hardest* part of a show or a role you may be working on.
- Find a quiet, comfortable place to sit, and try to imagine yourself feeling your most ideal feelings about your performance. Do you believe this is actually possible and achievable? Close your eyes

and commit to feeling these feelings. Breathe in the positive feeling on every inhalation, letting go of any negative feelings or doubt on every exhalation.

- Keep your eyes closed and begin to specifically imagine every step of your performance. Make sure you keep committing to seeing yourself successfully performing every task. This may prove very challenging, but don't open your eyes until you've really walked yourself through the entire performance in your imagination. How did this feel to you? Do you believe this is actually possible? Does it make you feel more confident and excited about your performance?
- Now imagine the way you would like to feel after your successful, ideal performance. Take the time to see imaginary events, perhaps the recognition of your teachers, peers, and loved ones. More importantly, how did this make you feel about *yourself*? Visualization is a powerful tool in manifesting even your wildest, most audacious dreams.

# VIDEO RESOURCES

To view a particular video, go to https://vimeo.com/channels/1392853.

| VIDEO NUMBER | LOCATION IN BOOK | VIDEO TITLE | OPENING LINES | Run Time |
|---|---|---|---|---|
| 1 | **Introduction** | Welcome to *The Singer Acts, the Actor Sings* | Welcome to *The Singer Acts, the Actor Sings.* | **2:02** |
| 2 | **Chapter 1** | What is Acting? | Let's talk about acting. | **1:27** |
| 3 | **Chapter 1: Exercise 2** | Finding the Action of the Scene | When you set foot on stage... | **3:47** |
| 4 | **Chapter 1: Exercise 3** | Finding Obstacles That Match Your Action | Whether they know it or not, when the audience... | **1:32** |
| 5 | **Chapter 1: Exercise 8** | Self-Directing with an Elevator Pitch | Every actor needs to learn how to self-direct. | **2:09** |
| 6 | **Chapter 1: Exercise 9** | Be Aware of Your Eyes | "I'm ready for my close-up, Mr. DeMille." | **2:01** |
| 7 | **Chapter 1: Exercise 10** | The Face | So let's talk about the awareness of our face... | **2:09** |
| 8 | **Chapter 1: Exercise 11** | Go to the Zero | You've probably heard someone tell you... | **2:04** |
| 9 | **Chapter 1: Exercise 14** | Playing Opposites | A lot of times when we watch great acting... | **2:57** |
| 10 | **Chapter 1: Exercise 15** | Breathe Before You Speak | I think you'll find it nearly impossible... | **2:06** |
| 11 | **Chapter 2** | What Is Singing? | "La la la la la la la." Is that singing? | **1:46** |
| 12 | **Introduction** | Living Through Song | Let's talk about living through song. | **1:32** |
| 13 | **Chapter 2: Page 35** | Legato | When you're acting and you're doing a play... | **2:52** |

| VIDEO NUMBER | LOCATION IN BOOK | VIDEO TITLE | OPENING LINES | Run Time |
|---|---|---|---|---|
| 14 | **Chapter 2: Page 35** | Integrate Your Thoughts and Music with the Legato Concept | We've covered the concept of legato... | **4:03** |
| 15 | **Chapter 2: Page 36** | Delay the Diphthong | Since we just covered primary vowels... | **3:02** |
| 16 | **Chapter 2: Page 43** | Sing with a Focused, Gathered Sound | Let's talk about a concept that I call... the vocal tract. | **4:49** |
| 17 | **Chapter 2: Page 43** | The Language of Singing via Open Sounds, i.e., Vowels | We're going to talk about the importance of vowels. | **3:16** |
| 18 | **Chapter 2: Page 48** | Support | Let's talk about the *appoggio*. | **2:01** |
| 19 | **Chapter 2: Page 81** | Integrate Your Thoughts and Music with the Legato Concept | We're going to continue with the concept of legato... | **3:21** |
| 20 | **Chapter 2: Exercise 17** | Use Slow-Motion Speech to Find Your Singing Voice | A great way to get yourself familiar with... | **3:07** |
| 21 | **Chapter 2: Exercise 19** | Disengage Your Tongue | Let's talk about a part of the body... | **3:30** |
| 22 | **Chapter 2: Exercise 21** | Closed and Open Vowels | Let's talk about vowels. | **5:10** |
| 23 | **Chapter 2: Exercise 22** | The Diaphragm | Let's talk about support. | **5:08** |
| 24 | **Chapter 2: Exercise 24** | Find Your Support with a Music Stand | So as fun as that was... | **3:57** |
| 25 | **Chapter 2: Exercise 25** | Find Your Support with Your Hand | So I think you're getting the idea... | **4:22** |
| 26 | **Chapter 2: Exercises 32 & 33** | Exercises to Find Your Natural Vibrato | Let's talk about vibrato. | **2:37** |
| | | | Total Time: | **72.87** |

# INDEX